Happy Cooking

Ollie

Enjoy!

Karel

Cherries Cafe

Secrets

Cherries Cafe Secrets

Published by Cherries Cafe
Copyright © 2006
Cherries Cafe
6000 Meadowbrook Mall, Suite 2
Clemmons, North Carolina 27012

This cookbook is a collection of favorite recipes,
which are not necessarily original recipes.

ISBN: 0-9771562-0-6

Edited, Designed, and Manufactured by
CommunityClassics™
An imprint of
FRP™
P.O. Box 305142
Nashville, Tennessee 37230
800-358-0560

Manufactured in China
First Printing: 2006 6,000 copies
Second Printing: 2007 4,000 copies

This book is dedicated to the memory
of the strong women in our lives.

Roxie W. Hunt

Myrten Cherry

Hilda Ketner

Preface

Cherries Cafe is steeped in tradition. Many of our recipes have been passed down from our family and friends. Our recipes are on scraps of paper, bridge tallies, and so forth, collected from friends, neighbors, and co-workers through the years. Some we have changed to suit our taste; others are our original recipes.

From early childhood, I have associated food with happy memories. As we were growing up on our small farm, most of our family gatherings centered around a shared meal. My mother was a great scratch cook. She never owned a cookbook; her knowledge was passed down from her mother and other ladies in the community. We truly lived off the land. She canned her vegetables and fruits in the summer, cured hams, and raised chickens that we could use all year.

She cooked out of necessity but seemed to enjoy it. Her food was served with love, and as a bonus, it tasted good. My love for cooking came from my mother. After many years of cooking for my family and entertaining friends, it seemed the right time to open Cherries Cafe.

My career in food started at the Ashlyn Hotel Dining Room in Asheboro, North Carolina, where I worked as a waitress in high school and college. In the early 1950s, the best restaurants were in hotels. We patterned Cherries Cafe after my memories of the hotel dining room.

ollie cherry

I suppose Cherries started for me as my mother's dream. I was at the stage in life where I wasn't sure which direction to go, with two boys, Reid and Zack, to raise.

Thank goodness for my mother's giant step in faith and that I am by her side. Now, Reid has joined us, making three generations at Cherries.

I can honestly say I love to come to work; it is so much more than cooking. At Cherries, I have made lifelong friends with my co-workers and customers.

We are family,

Karol McGill

I love to cook. That is what bonds Ollie, Karol, and me together. I have learned so much about food and life in my years here. Having Ollie for a teacher and a friend is a great blessing. Anyone in this business knows how hard the work is—long hours, hard floors, smiling when you really don't want to. Here we take the time to laugh together.

Watching the children grow is the real fun at Cherries. Karol's son, Zack, spent his entire first year in dry storage. Lindsey would help us with our tables at five years of age, and now she's waiting tables while attending college. Making gingerbread houses at Christmas is really amusing. The light in the children's eyes while decorating them could melt the heart of the biggest Scrooge. These are the things that make Cherries Cafe unique.

The words "thank you" can't touch how it feels when someone truly believes in you.

Donna Alexander

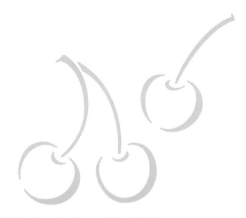

Acknowledgments

We are especially grateful to our friends and customers who have supported us for these sixteen years. Our thanks also go to our dedicated staff, who have been with us for years. They are efficient and loyal, and we love each of them.

Most of all, we appreciate Donna Alexander, who finally said, "Let's do it." She has worked hard to put this cookbook together for us. Our thanks to Kitty Smith for her proofing and editing.

We wish we could thank each of you, our customers, by name, but please know that you are special to us. We have been through births and deaths with you. We have laughed and cried with you. You are the heartbeat of Cherries.

Thank you,
Karol and ollie

History

What Cherries brings to the table—what separates us from other restaurants—is real Southern hospitality and great food. Ollie Cherry and her daughter, Karol McGill, own the restaurant. Their hard work and talent for cooking have created an inviting, elegant dining room and a devoted clientele. Their natural Southern charm, dedication, and love of community have built an amazing business.

Ollie and Karol started their business by catering from a small house on Stratford Road. No job was too big or too small. They carried food all over the state. The furniture market in High Point was the perfect showcase for Cherries' food. As the business grew, so did the need for a larger kitchen, resulting in the present-day Cherries Cafe. There was a line at the door the first day the cafe opened in 1989 and Cherries has been going strong ever since. Word of mouth was and is the best advertisement.

Karol starts each morning around 5 A.M., cooking chicken, making rolls, baking cakes and pies. As the morning progresses, the pace picks up. Ollie bounces into the kitchen with provisions needed for the day. The phone starts ringing, and the staff gradually appears. Mr. Cherry comes through the kitchen ("Hey, gurls!"), passing out our crisply pressed aprons. The door opens, and the customers roll in just as the final preparations are taking place. Lunch is about to begin.

With lunch in full swing, friends meet for business and pleasure. Conversation flows. The dining room is filled with warmth and hospitality. Customers chitchat, catching up on news, sharing pictures, or hashing out problems. Young friends grow up, and older friends pass on—the circle of life continues. If there is one word that describes the people of Cherries Cafe, it is *friend*. For all that we are, we genuinely love each other.

A common thread, whether in the past or present—on the road or in the dining room—is the quality fresh food. Everything is prepared from scratch. The freshest foods of the season are used in the selection of each day's menu. Local farmers provide fresh fruit and other produce whenever possible. Mr. Cherry goes to his hometown of Little Washington to meet the shrimp boat and visit the crab house, returning home with the best shrimp and crab meat. The customers stock their freezers with Cherries' goodies for future meals— shared or single.

Finally, remember:

Fresh is best, prepared with love and care—
always served with a smile!

Life has many happinesses.
Eating is the prime essential.
Then art—Works of Beauty—
nourishes the spirit
and warm friendship,
in ease and comfort,
fosters togetherness.
It is our Happiness
to serve you
all of these.

Author unknown

Table of Contents

*Brunch at cherries is always delightful—
a great start.*

Brunch at Cherries
is white tablecloths, fresh flowers,
and great food. Indoors or out, it is
the perfect way to celebrate any
occasion—an intimate gathering
place perfect for catching up or
conversation while sipping
mimosas or orange juice. Fresh
fruit, rich quiches, warm cinnamon
rolls, and buttery grits appear from
the kitchen. Steaming hot coffee
tops it off.

Brunch—it's more
than breakfast, less than lunch.
But more than that, it's a special
event at Cherries.

Brunch

Ham and Broccoli Strata

12 slices white bread, crusts removed and bread cut into cubes
1 (10-ounce) package frozen chopped broccoli, thawed and drained
2 cups diced cooked ham
6 eggs, beaten
3 1/4 cups milk
1 tablespoon dried onion flakes
1/4 teaspoon dry mustard
3 cups (12 ounces) shredded sharp Cheddar cheese

Layer the bread cubes, broccoli and ham in a buttered 8×12-inch baking dish. Combine the eggs, milk, onion flakes, dry mustard and cheese in a large bowl. Stir to mix well. Pour over the bread mixture. Cover and chill for at least 8 hours. Let stand at room temperature for 30 minutes before baking. Bake at 325 degrees for 55 to 60 minutes.

Baked Cheese Grits

4 cups water
1 teaspoon salt
1 cup grits
1 cup (4 ounces) shredded sharp Cheddar cheese
$1/2$ cup (1 stick) butter
1 teaspoon Worcestershire sauce
3 eggs, lightly beaten
Fresh parsley sprigs

Bring the water and salt to a boil in a saucepan. Stir in the grits. Cook for 30 minutes or until thick, stirring often. Remove from the heat and add the cheese, butter and Worcestershire sauce. Stir until the cheese and butter melt. Stir $1/4$ of the hot grits mixture gradually into the eggs in a bowl; stir the eggs back into the hot grits. Pour into a lightly greased 9-inch quiche dish. Bake at 350 degrees for 1 hour. Garnish with fresh parsley.

Brunch Sandwich

12 hard-cooked eggs, finely chopped
16 ounces Cheddar cheese, shredded
1/2 cup grated onion
3/4 cup mayonnaise
1 pound bacon, crisp-cooked and crumbled
1 1/2 teaspoons Worcestershire sauce
1/2 teaspoon pepper
1/2 teaspoon garlic powder
6 to 8 English muffins, split and lightly toasted
Grated Parmesan cheese

Combine the eggs, Cheddar cheese, onion, mayonnaise, bacon, Worcestershire sauce, pepper and garlic powder in a large bowl. Stir to mix well. Spoon onto the muffin halves. Sprinkle with Parmesan cheese. Arrange on a baking sheet. Bake at 350 degrees for 10 minutes or until hot and the cheese melts.

Muffin Tin Breakfast

6 slices bacon
6 eggs
Salt and pepper to taste
1 tablespoon butter, cut into 6 pieces
1/4 cup half-and half

Cook the bacon in a skillet until almost done. Remove to paper towels to drain. Cut 1 inch from 1 bacon slice and place in the bottom of a muffin cup. Wrap the remainder of the slice around the inside of the cup. Repeat with the remaining bacon. Break 1 egg into each muffin cup. Season with salt and pepper. Top each with a piece of butter. Pour 2 teaspoons of half-and-half over each egg. Bake at 350 degrees for 15 to 20 minutes or until the eggs are set and cooked through.

Creamed Eggs on Toast

1/2 cup (1 stick) butter
1/3 cup all-purpose flour
2 cups milk
1/4 teaspoon salt
1/4 teaspoon pepper
12 hard-cooked eggs, chopped and chilled
12 slices bread, toasted

Combine the butter and flour in the top of a double boiler. Cook over simmering water until smooth, stirring constantly. Stir in the milk, salt and pepper. Cook until thickened, stirring often. Pour over the chopped eggs in a bowl. Stir to mix well. Spread the egg mixture over the bread slices, covering to the edge. Arrange on a baking sheet. Broil until hot and bubbly, watching closely so that the edges don't burn. Serve immediately.

Bacon and Cheese Bites

1 cup shredded Swiss cheese
8 slices bacon, crisp-cooked and crumbled
3 tablespoons mayonnaise
1 tablespoon chopped onion
1/2 teaspoon celery seeds
1 loaf sliced party rye bread

Combine the cheese, bacon, mayonnaise, onion and celery seeds in a bowl. Stir to mix well. Spread on the bread slices and arrange on a baking sheet. Broil until hot and bubbly. Serve immediately.

Note: This is great for brunch or as an appetizer.

Cream Cheese Braid

1 cup sour cream
1/2 cup granulated sugar
1 teaspoon salt
1/2 cup (1 stick) butter, melted
2 envelopes dry yeast
1/2 cup warm water
  (105 to 110 degrees)

2 eggs, beaten
4 cups all-purpose flour
Cream Cheese Filling
2 cups confectioners' sugar
1/4 cup milk
2 teaspoons vanilla extract

Heat the sour cream in a saucepan over low heat. Stir in the sugar, salt and butter. Remove from the heat and let cool to lukewarm. Sprinkle the yeast over the warm water in a large bowl. Stir until the yeast dissolves. Add the sour cream mixture, eggs, and flour. Stir to mix well. Cover tightly and chill overnight. Divide the dough into 4 portions. Roll out each portion on a floured work surface to an 8×12-inch rectangle. Spread each with 1/4 of the Cream Cheese Filling. Roll up from the long side. Pinch the seam to seal and fold the edges under. Place the rolls, seam side down, on a greased baking sheet. Make slits with a sharp knife every 2 inches, cutting 2/3 of the way through. Cover and let rise in a warm place until doubled in bulk. Bake at 375 degrees for 12 to 15 minutes. Remove to a wire rack. Combine the confectioners' sugar, milk and vanilla in a bowl. Stir until smooth. Drizzle over the warm braids.

Cream Cheese Filling

24 ounces cream cheese, softened
3/4 cup sugar
1 egg, beaten

2 teaspoons vanilla extract
1/8 teaspoon salt

Combine the cream cheese, sugar, egg, vanilla and salt in a bowl. Beat with an electric mixer at low speed until smooth and creamy.

Cinnamon Cream Cheese Sticks

Serves 10 to 12

16 ounces cream cheese, softened
1 teaspoon vanilla extract
1 egg yolk
1 loaf bread, crusts removed
1 cup sugar
2 tablespoons ground cinnamon
1 cup (2 sticks) butter, melted

Beat the cream cheese, vanilla and egg yolk in a bowl until smooth. Flatten the bread slices on a work surface. Spread with the cream cheese mixture. Combine the sugar and cinnamon in a shallow dish. Stir to mix well. Dip the coated bread in the melted butter and then coat in the cinnamon-sugar. Cut into strips and arrange on a buttered baking sheet. Bake at 350 degrees for 10 minutes. Remove to a wire rack to cool.

Note: These can be made ahead and frozen before baking.

Flagship Rum Rolls

1 cup milk

1/4 cup granulated sugar

1/4 cup shortening

1/8 teaspoon salt

1 cake yeast or 1 envelope dry yeast

1 egg, beaten

1 1/2 teaspoons rum extract

3 1/2 cups all-purpose flour, sifted

2 tablespoons butter, melted

1/4 cup granulated sugar

1/2 cup raisins, chopped

1 cup confectioners' sugar

2 tablespoons hot water

Scald the milk in a saucepan over low heat. Pour over the sugar, shortening and salt in a large bowl. Let cool to lukewarm. Add the yeast and stir to dissolve. Let stand for 10 minutes. Add the egg, rum extract and 1/2 the flour. Whisk until smooth. Stir in the remaining flour; the dough should be soft but not sticky. Cover with a towel and let rise in a warm place for 1 1/2 hours or until doubled in bulk. Punch down the dough and divide in half. Cover 1/2 and place the remaining dough on a floured work surface. Roll out to a 4×12-inch rectangle, 1/2 inch thick. Brush with 1/2 the melted butter. Sprinkle with 1/2 the 1/4 cup sugar and 1/2 the raisins. Roll up from the long side. Pinch the seam to seal. Repeat with the remaining dough, melted butter, sugar and raisins. Cut the rolls into 18 slices and place in greased muffin cups. Let rise for 30 minutes or until doubled in bulk. Bake at 400 degrees for 15 to 20 minutes. Mix the confectioners' sugar and hot water in a bowl. Brush over the hot rolls.

Bacon Biscuit Cups

6 ounces cream cheese, softened
2 tablespoons milk
1 egg
1/2 cup shredded Swiss cheese
1 green onion, chopped
1 (10-count) can refrigerator flaky biscuits
5 slices bacon, crisp-cooked and crumbled
Chopped green onions

Combine the cream cheese, milk and egg in a bowl. Beat with an electric mixer at medium speed until smooth. Stir in the Swiss cheese and 1 green onion. Separate the biscuits and place on a work surface. Pat each biscuit into a 5-inch circle. Press each circle into a greased muffin cup, forming a 1/4-inch rim at the top. Sprinkle 1/2 the bacon into the muffin cups. Spoon the cream cheese mixture onto the bacon. Bake at 375 degrees for 22 minutes or until set. Sprinkle with the remaining bacon and garnish with chopped green onions.

whipping Cream Biscuits

2 cups self-rising flour
1/4 cup (1/2 stick) butter, melted
3/4 to 1 cup heavy cream
1/4 cup (1/2 stick) butter, melted

Mix the flour and 1/4 cup melted butter in a bowl. Stir in the cream just until moistened. Turn out onto a floured work surface and knead 3 or 4 times. Roll or pat out the dough. Cut with a biscuit cutter. Arrange on an ungreased baking sheet with the edges not quite touching. Bake at 350 degrees for 12 to 15 minutes or until golden brown. Brush the hot biscuits with 1/4 cup melted butter.

Bran Muffins

1 (15-ounce) box wheat bran flakes cereal with raisins
5 cups all-purpose flour
3 cups sugar
5 teaspoons baking soda
2 teaspoons salt
4 eggs, beaten
4 cups buttermilk
1 cup shortening, melted

Mix the bran flakes, flour, sugar, baking soda and salt in a large bowl. Make a well in the center and pour in the eggs, buttermilk and shortening. Stir just until moistened. Cover and chill for at least 24 hours or up to 6 weeks. Fill greased muffin cups 2/3 full. Bake at 350 degrees for 20 minutes. Remove to a wire rack to cool.

Banana Crumb Muffins

1 1/2 cups all-purpose flour
1 teaspoon baking soda
1 teaspoon baking powder
1/2 teaspoon salt
3 large bananas, mashed
3/4 cup sugar
1 egg, lightly beaten

5 1/3 tablespoons butter or
    margarine, melted
1/3 cup packed light brown sugar
1 tablespoon all-purpose flour
1/8 teaspoon ground cinnamon
1 tablespoon butter or
    margarine, softened

Mix 1 1/2 cups flour, the baking soda, baking powder and salt in a large bowl. Mix the bananas, sugar, egg and 5 1/3 tablespoons melted butter in a bowl. Add to the dry ingredients and stir just until moistened. Fill greased or paper-lined muffin cups 3/4 full. Mix the brown sugar, 1 tablespoon flour and the cinnamon in a bowl. Cut in 1 tablespoon butter with a pastry blender or fork until crumbly. Sprinkle over the muffins.   Bake at 375 degrees for 18 to 20 minutes or until a wooden pick inserted in the center comes out clean. Cool in the pan for 10 minutes. Remove to a wire rack to cool.

Blueberry Streusel Muffins

2 1/3 cups all-purpose flour
4 teaspoons baking powder
1/2 teaspoon salt
1/4 cup (1/2 stick) butter or
    margarine, softened
1/3 cup sugar
1 egg
1 cup milk

1 teaspoon vanilla extract
1 1/2 cups fresh or frozen blueberries
1/2 cup sugar
1/3 cup all-purpose flour
1/2 teaspoon ground cinnamon
1/4 cup (1/2 stick) butter or
    margarine, softened

Mix 2 1/3 cups flour, the baking powder and salt together. Beat 1/4 cup butter in a large bowl with an electric mixer at medium speed until smooth. Beat in 1/3 cup sugar gradually. Beat until light and fluffy. Beat in the egg. Beat in the dry ingredients alternately with the milk. Stir in the vanilla. Fold in the blueberries. Fill greased muffin cups 2/3 full. Mix 1/2 cup sugar, 1/3 cup flour and the cinnamon in a bowl. Cut in 1/4 cup butter with a pastry blender or fork until crumbly. Sprinkle over the muffins. Bake at 375 degrees for 25 to 30 minutes or until golden brown. Remove to a wire rack to cool.

Crepes

3 eggs
1 1/2 cups milk
2 tablespoons vegetable oil
1 1/2 cups all-purpose flour
1/8 teaspoon salt

Beat the eggs in a bowl. Beat in the milk and oil gradually. Beat in the flour and salt gradually. Beat until smooth. Cover and chill for at least 2 hours or overnight. Stir the batter to mix. Ladle 2 tablespoons of batter into a lightly greased heated crepe pan. Tilt the pan to spread the batter thinly. Cook until light brown on both sides. Remove the crepe to waxed paper and repeat to use all the batter, stacking the cooked crepes on waxed paper.

Quiche Crust

4 ounces cream cheese, softened
$^1/_2$ cup (1 stick) butter, softened
2 cups all-purpose flour

Beat the cream cheese and butter in a bowl until smooth. Stir in the flour. Press into a lightly greased quiche dish. Cover and chill.

catawba punch

2 bottles white grape juice, well chilled
1 large bottle lemon-lime soda or ginger ale, well chilled
1 bottle club soda, well chilled
Champagne, well-chilled (optional)

Pour the grape juice, lemon-lime soda and club soda over ice in a punch bowl. Add Champagne. Stir to mix.

Note: This is the color of vintage Champagne.

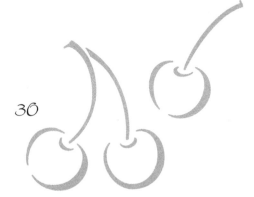

Orange Sherbet Punch

2 packages strawberry gelatin
2 cups boiling water
1 1/2 cups sugar
2 cups cold water
1 large can pineapple juice
1 large can orange juice
1 cup lemon juice
2 quarts orange sherbet
1 bottle ginger ale

Dissolve the gelatin in the boiling water in a large bowl. Add the sugar and stir until the sugar dissolves. Stir in the cold water. Mix the pineapple juice, orange juice and lemon juice together in a bowl. Add the gelatin mixture and stir to mix well. Cover and chill. Spoon the sherbet into the gelatin mixture. Stir in the ginger ale just before serving.

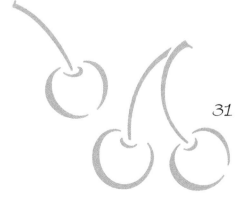

Spiced Percolator Punch

2 1/4 cups pineapple juice
2 cups cranberry juice cocktail
1 3/4 cups water
1/2 cup packed brown sugar
3 cinnamon sticks, broken
1 tablespoon whole cloves
1 1/2 teaspoons whole allspice

Pour the pineapple juice, cranberry juice cocktail and water in the base of a coffee percolator. Place the brown sugar, cinnamon sticks, cloves and allspice in the clean basket and set in the percolator. Run through a standard cycle and serve hot.

Homemade V-8 Juice

1 bushel ripe tomatoes, quartered
5 large onions, chopped
5 large green bell peppers, chopped
1 bunch celery, chopped
1 1/2 cups chopped hot chiles
Salt
Sugar
1/2 jar horseradish
2/3 small bottle Worcestershire sauce

Combine the tomatoes, onions, bell peppers, celery and chiles in a very large saucepan. Cook until soft. Run through a juicer or food mill or purée in a food processor and strain through a mesh sieve. Measure the juice and pour into a very large bowl. Add 1 teaspoon salt and 1 teaspoon sugar for every 4 cups of juice. Stir in the horseradish and Worcestershire sauce.

Note: This juice can be frozen for up to 6 months.

*High Tea at Cherries is always festive —
a memorable occasion.*

High Tea days are
always electric, frenzied, and fun.
The aroma of cakes and scones fills
the air. Silver platters of luscious
food cover the table to overflowing.
The silver tea urn sparkles, surrounded
by our collection of teapots.

Guests appear in
their finest "Sunday best." Friendly
conversation pervades the room,
along with the smell of spiced cider.
Family and neighbors take the time to
enjoy each other. Taking time for tea
is nourishing to your body and spirit,
and a delightful way to spend an
afternoon at Cherries!

High Tea

The custom of afternoon tea originated in England in the early eighteenth century. When the Duchess of Bedford got too hungry to wait until dinner, she demanded an afternoon tea with biscuits and cakes, a habit other ladies adopted.

Tea became a way for middle and upper middle classes to entertain, usually around three o'clock to five o'clock in the afternoon. High tea can serve as a meal with hearty dishes such as tiny muffins, scones, crumpets, salmon, cheeses, pound cake, and sometimes a roast chicken, pork, or beef.

Times have changed. Once associated with ladies wearing white gloves and hats, tea is now heartier. Afternoon tea is a way to have a light meal and enjoy a nice social event with friends and business associates.

Party Meatballs

3 pounds ground beef
1 cup bread crumbs
2 or 3 eggs
Salt and pepper to taste
Garlic salt to taste
4$^1/_2$ cups grape jelly
2 bottles chili sauce

Combine the ground beef, bread crumbs and eggs in a bowl. Season with salt, pepper and garlic salt. Stir to mix well. Shape into small balls and arrange on a baking sheet. Bake at 350 degrees for 30 minutes or until cooked through. Remove to paper towels to drain. Mix the jelly and chili sauce in a saucepan. Bring to a boil, stirring often. Pour into a baking dish. Add the meatballs and stir gently to mix. Bake at 350 degrees for 15 to 20 minutes. Serve immediately.

curried Chicken Balls

6 ounces cream cheese, softened
2 tablespoons orange marmalade
2 teaspoons curry powder
3/4 teaspoon salt
1/4 teaspoon pepper
3 cups finely chopped cooked chicken
3 tablespoons finely chopped celery
3 tablespoons finely chopped onion
1 cup finely chopped almonds

Combine the cream cheese, marmalade, curry powder, salt and pepper in a large bowl. Stir to mix well. Stir in the chicken, celery and onion. Shape into 1-inch balls and roll in the almonds. Arrange on a serving platter. Cover and chill.

Note: Faye gave us this recipe many years ago.

Layered Crab Dish

8 ounces (or more) cream cheese, softened
Chopped green onions
1 tablespoon Worcestershire sauce
1 cup ketchup, chili sauce or cocktail sauce
1 tablespoon horseradish
Hot red pepper sauce to taste
1 pound fresh lump or back-fin crab meat, drained and flaked
Chopped fresh parsley

       Spread the cream cheese on a serving dish or fish-shaped serving plate. Cover with green onions. Drizzle with the Worcestershire sauce. Mix the ketchup and horseradish in a bowl. Season with hot sauce. Spread over the green onions. Cover with the crab meat and sprinkle with chopped parsley. Serve with crackers.

crab Triangles

1 cup crab meat, drained
1 jar Old English cheese spread
1/2 cup (1 stick) margarine, softened
1 tablespoon mayonnaise
1/2 teaspoon garlic powder
1/2 teaspoon seasoned salt
6 English muffins, split

Combine the crab meat, cheese spread, margarine, mayonnaise, garlic powder and seasoned salt in a bowl. Stir to mix well. Spread onto the muffin halves. Place on a baking sheet and freeze until firm. Cut each muffin half into 8 wedges. Arrange on a baking sheet. Bake at 350 degrees for 10 minutes or until hot. Serve immediately.

Note: These can be made up to 1 week ahead. Cut into wedges and bake when ready to serve.

Great Cheese Ball

16 ounces cream cheese, softened
1 envelope dried onion soup mix
2 teaspoons Worcestershire sauce
1 teaspoon lemon juice
8 ounces Cheddar cheese, shredded
8 ounces Pepper Jack cheese, shredded
Chopped pecans or sunflower seeds

Combine the cream cheese, soup mix, Worcestershire sauce and lemon juice in a bowl. Stir to mix well. Add the Cheddar cheese and Pepper Jack cheese and stir to mix well. Shape into a ball and roll in chopped pecans. Cover and chill. Serve with crackers.

cheese Ring with Strawberry preserves   Serves 20

16 ounces sharp Cheddar cheese, shredded
1 cup pecans, chopped
3/4 cup mayonnaise
1 onion, grated
1 garlic clove, pressed
1/2 teaspoon Tabasco sauce
1 cup strawberry preserves

Combine the cheese, pecans, mayonnaise, onion, garlic and Tabasco in a bowl. Stir to mix well. Shape into a ring on a serving plate. Spoon the preserves into the center.

Note: This recipe has been around for ages. It is really delicious.

Four-Layer Cheese Loaf

8 ounces sharp Cheddar cheese, shredded

1/2 cup mayonnaise

1/2 cup toasted chopped pecans

1 (10-ounce) package frozen chopped spinach, thawed, drained and squeezed dry

4 ounces cream cheese, softened

1/4 teaspoon salt

1/2 teaspoon pepper

4 ounces cream cheese, softened

1/4 cup chutney

1/4 teaspoon nutmeg

Toasted chopped pecans

Mix the Cheddar cheese, mayonnaise and 1/2 cup pecans in a bowl. Spread 1/2 the mixture in a 5×9-inch loaf pan lined with plastic wrap. Mix the spinach, 4 ounces cream cheese, salt and pepper in a bowl. Spread evenly over the Cheddar cheese layer in the pan. Mix 4 ounces cream cheese, the chutney and nutmeg in a bowl. Spread evenly over the spinach layer. Spread the remaining Cheddar cheese mixture evenly over the chutney layer. Chill, covered, until firm. Invert onto a serving plate and remove the plastic wrap. Sprinkle with toasted chopped pecans and serve with crackers.

Southwest Appetizer Cheesecake

Serves 16

2/3 cup finely crushed tortilla chips

2 tablespoons margarine, melted

1 cup cottage cheese

24 ounces cream cheese, softened

4 eggs

10 ounces sharp Cheddar cheese, shredded

1 (4-ounce) can chopped green chiles, drained

1 (8-ounce) container jalapeño Cheddar cheese dip

1 cup sour cream

1 cup chopped tomato

1/2 cup chopped green onions

1/4 cup sliced black olives

Sour cream

Mix the crushed tortilla chips and melted margarine in a bowl. Press into the bottom of a 9-inch springform pan. Bake at 325 degrees for 15 minutes. Remove to a wire rack to cool. Process the cottage cheese in a food processor until smooth. Remove to a large bowl. Add the cream cheese and beat until smooth. Add the eggs, 1 at a time, beating well after each addition. Stir in the Cheddar cheese and green chiles. Pour over the baked crust. Bake at 325 degrees for 1 hour. Mix the dip and 1 cup sour cream together in a bowl. Spread over the cheesecake. Bake for 10 minutes longer. Remove to a wire rack. Loosen from the side of the pan with a sharp knife. Let cool completely and remove the side. Cover and chill. Top with the tomato, green onions, olives and sour cream. Serve with crackers.

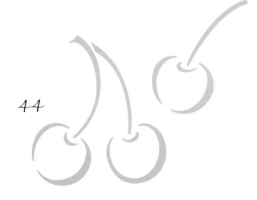

Cheese Biscuits

1 cup (2 sticks) margarine, softened
8 ounces sharp Cheddar cheese, shredded
2 cups all-purpose flour
$1/2$ teaspoon salt
$3/4$ teaspoon cayenne pepper
$2^1/2$ cups crisp rice cereal

Mix the margarine and cheese together in a large bowl. Stir in the flour, salt and cayenne pepper. Fold in the cereal gently with your hands; the mixture will be stiff. Shape into 1-inch balls. Place 1 inch apart on a greased baking sheet. Flatten the balls with the back of a fork to make a crisscross pattern. Bake at 350 degrees for 15 to 20 minutes or until the edges begin to brown. Remove to a wire rack to cool. The biscuits will be crisp when cool.

Note: This is a great recipe that has been around for years. Sometimes you just can't improve on the original.

Scones

2 cups self-rising flour
$1/2$ cup sugar
2 teaspoons grated orange zest
$5^1/3$ tablespoons butter
$1/2$ cup pecans
$1/2$ cup buttermilk
$1/4$ cup fresh orange juice
1 teaspoon vanilla extract
Sugar

Mix the flour, $1/2$ cup sugar and the orange zest in a bowl. Cut in the butter with a pastry blender or fork until crumbly. Add the pecans, buttermilk, orange juice and vanilla. Stir just until moistened. Turn out onto a floured work surface and knead for 3 to 4 minutes. Divide the dough in half. Pat out each $1/2$ of the dough into a circle on a greased baking sheet sprinkled with sugar. Chill for 30 minutes. Bake at 350 degrees for 15 minutes or until golden brown. Remove to a wire rack to cool. Cut into wedges.

cucumber sandwiches

2 loaves extra-thin sliced bread
8 ounces cream cheese, softened
2 pickling cucumbers, peeled and finely chopped
8 drops Tabasco sauce
$1/4$ teaspoon garlic powder
$1/4$ teaspoon pepper
Salt to taste
3 to 4 pickling cucumbers, thinly sliced
Chopped fresh dillweed

Remove the crusts from the bread and cut out rounds with a biscuit cutter. Cover and keep moist. Combine the cream cheese, chopped cucumbers, Tabasco, garlic powder and pepper in a bowl. Season with salt. Stir gently to mix. Spread on the bread rounds. Top with the sliced cucumbers and sprinkle with dillweed. Serve immediately.

Note: The spread can be made up to 4 hours ahead. Be sure to use small pickling cucumbers for better flavor.

vegetable pinwheels

16 ounces cream cheese, softened
1 package ranch salad dressing mix
2 green onions, finely chopped
4 flour tortillas
1/2 cup chopped red bell pepper
1/2 cup diced celery
1 tall can black olives, drained and chopped

Combine the cream cheese, salad dressing mix and green onions in a bowl. Stir to mix well. Spread on the tortillas. Top with the bell pepper, celery and olives. Roll up tightly and wrap in waxed paper. Chill for at least 2 hours or overnight. Cut into slices and arrange on a serving plate. Store any leftovers in an airtight container in the refrigerator.

Stuffed Mushrooms

1 (10-ounce) package frozen
  chopped spinach
30 to 36 large fresh mushrooms
1/2 cup (1 stick) butter, melted
1 onion, finely chopped
1/2 cup bread crumbs
1/2 teaspoon garlic powder

1 teaspoon salt
1/4 teaspoon pepper
1/2 teaspoon nutmeg
1/8 teaspoon dry mustard
1 cup sour cream
Grated Parmesan cheese

Cook the spinach in a saucepan of boiling unsalted water according to the package directions. Drain and squeeze dry. Remove the stems from the mushrooms and chop the stems. Melt the butter in a large skillet. Add the mushroom caps and sauté for 5 to 10 minutes. Remove with tongs and arrange on a baking sheet. Add the onion to the skillet and sauté until tender. Add the chopped mushroom stems and sauté until tender. Remove from the heat and add the bread crumbs, garlic powder, salt, pepper, nutmeg, dry mustard and sour cream. Stir to mix well. Spoon into the mushroom caps. Sprinkle with Parmesan cheese. Bake at 375 degrees for 15 minutes.

Note: This is another one of Karen's recipes.

Green Grapes with Sour Cream

1 pound seedless green grapes
$^3/_4$ cup sour cream
$^1/_4$ cup packed brown sugar
Grated zest of 1 orange

Place the grapes in a bowl or shallow baking dish. Spread the sour cream over the grapes and sprinkle with the brown sugar. Cover and chill for 1 to 2 hours or until the brown sugar dissolves into the sour cream. Sprinkle with the orange zest.

Praline Pecans

1¹/₂ cups chopped pecans
¹/₄ cup packed brown sugar
2 tablespoons heavy cream

Mix the pecans, brown sugar and cream in a bowl. Spread in a lightly buttered 9-inch baking pan. Bake at 350 degrees for 20 minutes, stirring once halfway through baking. Remove from the oven and stir. Let cool completely and store in an airtight container.

*Chicken at cherries is always fresh—
a comfort food.*

Chicken is a staple at Cherries, yielding lots of fresh meat and stock, which makes everything taste better. We start cooking chicken before sunup, and it goes on all day. I wouldn't want to be a chicken within one hundred miles of Cherries Cafe.

Chicken is consistently the entrée of choice for our customers. Many people take comfort from eating a dish of Creamy Crunchy Chicken. Our chick'n pick'n is done by loving, tender hands, which adds a flavor all its own. You can really taste the difference at Cherries.

Chicken

ollie's chicken casserole

3 cups chopped cooked chicken breasts
1 package long grain and wild rice mix,
   cooked according to the package
   directions
1 (16-ounce) package frozen
   French-style green beans, cooked
   and drained
1 cup mayonnaise

1 (10-ounce) can condensed cream of
   mushroom soup
1 can water chestnuts, drained
   and chopped
1 teaspoon pepper
1/2 cup sliced almonds
Paprika

     Combine the chicken, rice mix, beans, mayonnaise, mushroom soup, water chestnuts and pepper in a large bowl. Stir to mix well. Spoon into a greased 11×13-inch baking dish. Sprinkle with the almonds and paprika. Bake at 350 degrees for 30 minutes or until bubbly.

Creamy Crunchy Chicken

Serves 6

4 boneless skinless chicken breasts, cooked and shredded
1 cup sour cream
2 (10-ounce) cans condensed cream of chicken soup

1 teaspoon pepper
1 sleeve butter crackers, crushed
2 teaspoons poppy seeds
3 tablespoons butter, melted

Combine the chicken, sour cream, chicken soup and pepper in a large bowl. Stir to mix well. Spoon into a 9×13-inch baking dish. Sprinkle with the crushed crackers and poppy seeds. Drizzle with the melted butter. Bake at 350 degrees for 20 minutes or until bubbly.

Chicken Divan

Serves 6

1 bunch fresh broccoli, chopped and lightly steamed
2 cups chopped cooked chicken breasts
$2/3$ cup sour cream
$1/3$ cup mayonnaise

2 teaspoons lemon juice
$1/2$ cup (2 ounces) grated Parmesan cheese
Paprika

Spread the broccoli on the bottom of a well greased 9×11-inch baking dish. Arrange the chicken on top. Mix the sour cream, mayonnaise and lemon juice in a bowl. Pour evenly over the chicken. Sprinkle with the Parmesan cheese and paprika. Bake at 350 degrees for 30 minutes or until bubbly.

Tomato Basil Chicken

1 package chicken flavor Rice-A-Roni
2 cups chopped cooked chicken
1 teaspoon basil
2 cups broccoli florets
1 tomato, seeded and chopped
1 cup (4 ounces) shredded mozzarella cheese

Prepare the Rice-A-Roni, following the range top directions on the package through Step 2. Reduce the heat and simmer for 10 minutes. Stir in the chicken, basil, broccoli and tomato. Simmer, covered, for 5 to 10 minutes or until the liquid is absorbed. Sprinkle with the cheese and serve.

chicken Tortilla Bake

2 (10-ounce) cans condensed cream of
  mushroom soup
1 cup sour cream
2 cups chopped cooked chicken
1 (4-ounce) can chopped green chiles
1 onion, chopped
1 1/2 cups (6 ounces) shredded
  Cheddar cheese
1 tablespoon chili powder

1 teaspoon cumin
Salt to taste
Pepper to taste
Garlic salt to taste
4 large flour tortillas
1/2 cup (2 ounces) shredded
  Cheddar cheese
Diced tomato
Diced avocado

Combine the mushroom soup, sour cream, chicken, green chiles, onion, 1 1/2 cups cheese, chili powder and cumin in a large bowl. Season with salt, pepper and garlic salt. Stir to mix well. Fit 1 tortilla in the bottom of a 10-inch springform pan. Spread 1/3 of the chicken mixture on the tortilla. Top with another tortilla and 1/3 of the chicken mixture. Top with another tortilla and the remaining chicken mixture. Top with the remaining tortilla and sprinkle with 1/2 cup cheese. Bake at 350 degrees for 30 minutes or until bubbly. Remove to a wire rack. Loosen from the side of the pan with a sharp knife and remove the side. Top with chopped tomato and avocado. Cut into wedges.

chicken Bacon Bake

6 boneless chicken breasts, cut into
   1-inch cubes
Garlic powder to taste
Seasoned salt to taste
1 tablespoon vegetable oil
1/2 cup all-purpose flour
2 cups milk
2 cups heavy cream
Salt and pepper to taste
16 ounces fettuccini, cooked al dente
   and drained

1 cup sautéed fresh mushrooms or
   canned mushrooms
6 green onions, chopped
12 slices bacon, crisp-cooked
   and crumbled
1/2 cup (2 ounces) shredded white
   Cheddar cheese
1/2 cup (2 ounces) shredded yellow
   Cheddar cheese
1/4 cup (1 ounce) grated
   Parmesan cheese

Season the chicken with garlic powder and seasoned salt. Heat the oil in a skillet. Add the chicken and brown on both sides. Remove the chicken to a plate using a slotted spoon. Add the flour to the skillet. Cook for 1 minute, stirring constantly. Stir in the milk and cream. Cook until thick, stirring constantly. Add the chicken. Season with salt and pepper. Divide the pasta among 6 individual ramekins. Top with the chicken and sauce. Sprinkle with the mushrooms, green onions, bacon, white Cheddar cheese, yellow Cheddar cheese and Parmesan cheese. Bake at 350 degrees for 10 minutes or until the cheese melts. Serve immediately.

chicken Tetrazzini

1 cup water
1/4 teaspoon salt
1/8 teaspoon pepper
4 boneless chicken breasts, cut into
   1/2-inch cubes
1 tablespoon vegetable oil
1 package spaghetti
1/4 cup (1/2 stick) butter
1 green bell pepper, chopped
2 1/2 tablespoons all-purpose flour
1 cup milk
1/4 cup dry white wine
1 (10-ounce) can condensed cream
   of mushroom soup

1 (4-ounce) can sliced mushrooms,
   drained
1 (2-ounce) jar sliced pimento, drained
1/8 teaspoon garlic powder
2 cups (8 ounces) shredded Cheddar
   cheese
1/2 cup (2 ounces) grated
   Parmesan cheese
1/2 cup sliced almonds, toasted
1 cup (4 ounces) shredded
   Cheddar cheese

Bring the water, salt and pepper to a boil in a saucepan. Add the chicken and reduce the heat. Cook, covered, for 10 minutes or until the chicken is cooked through. Drain well and set aside. Add the oil to a large saucepan of boiling salted water. Add the pasta and cook until al dente; drain. Melt the butter in a large saucepan. Add the bell pepper and sauté until tender. Stir in the flour. Cook for 1 minute, stirring constantly. Stir in the milk, wine, mushroom soup, mushrooms, pimentos, garlic powder, 2 cups Cheddar cheese, the Parmesan cheese and chicken. Cook until thickened, stirring constantly. Server over the spaghetti and sprinkle with the almonds and 1 cup Cheddar cheese.

chicken crepes

3 cups finely chopped cooked chicken
1 cup (4 ounces) freshly grated
    Parmesan cheese
1 tablespoon butter or margarine
4 ounces finely chopped
    fresh mushrooms
1/2 teaspoon salt
1/4 teaspoon pepper
1/4 teaspoon nutmeg

5 1/3 tablespoons butter or margarine
1/3 cup all-purpose flour
3 cups milk
1 cup heavy cream
1/4 cup medium-dry sherry (or to taste)
1 recipe Crepes (page 28)
1/2 cup (2 ounces) freshly grated
    Parmesan cheese

Mix the chicken and 1 cup Parmesan cheese in a large
bowl. Melt 1 tablespoon butter in a skillet. Add the mushrooms and sauté until tender.
Stir in the salt, pepper and nutmeg. Add to the chicken mixture. Melt 5 1/3 tablespoons
butter in a heavy saucepan over low heat. Stir in the flour. Cook for 1 minute, stirring
constantly. Stir in the milk gradually. Cook over medium heat until thick and bubbly,
stirring constantly. Stir in the cream and sherry. Reserve 1 cup of the sauce and add the
remaining sauce to the chicken mixture. Stir to mix well. Lay the crepes on a work
surface. Spoon 1/3 cup of the chicken mixture onto the center of each crepe. Roll up
tightly and arrange in a baking dish. Top with the reserved sauce and sprinkle with
1/2 cup Parmesan cheese. Bake at 350 degrees for 20 minutes or until hot.

chicken in pastry

2 cups chopped cooked chicken
1/2 cup chopped mushrooms
3 ounces cream cheese, softened
2 tablespoons butter, softened
1/2 cup water chestnuts, sliced
1 teaspoon lemon pepper
1 (8-count) can refrigerator
   crescent rolls

1/2 cup finely chopped pecans
1/2 cup seasoned stuffing mix
3 tablespoons butter, melted
1 (10-ounce) can condensed cream
   of mushroom soup
1 cup sour cream
1 teaspoon dillweed

Combine the chicken, mushrooms, cream cheese, 2 tablespoons butter, water chestnuts and lemon pepper in a bowl. Stir to mix well. Separate the crescent rolls on a work surface and press gently to flatten. Spoon 1/4 cup of the chicken mixture onto the center of each roll. Fold the dough over the filling and pinch the seams to seal. Mix the pecans and stuffing mix in a shallow dish. Pour 3 tablespoons melted butter into a shallow bowl. Dip the chicken rolls in the melted butter and coat in the pecan mixture. Arrange in a baking dish. Bake at 375 degrees for 20 minutes or until light brown. Mix the mushroom soup, sour cream and dillweed in a saucepan. Heat until hot, do not let boil. Serve over the chicken rolls.

chicken pecan quiche

1 cup all-purpose flour
1 cup (4 ounces) shredded sharp
   Cheddar cheese
3/4 cup pecans, chopped
1/2 teaspoon salt
1/4 teaspoon paprika
1/3 cup vegetable oil
3 eggs, beaten
1 cup sour cream

1/4 cup mayonnaise
1/2 cup chicken broth
2 cups chopped cooked chicken
1/2 cup (2 ounces) shredded sharp
   Cheddar cheese
1/4 cup finely chopped onion
1/4 teaspoon dillweed
3 drops hot red pepper sauce
1/4 cup pecan halves

     Combine the flour, 1 cup cheese, 3/4 cup pecans, the salt and paprika in a bowl. Stir to mix well. Stir in the oil. Reserve 1/4 of the mixture and press the remainder onto the bottom and up the side of a 9-inch quiche dish. Bake at 350 degrees for 10 minutes. Remove to a wire rack to cool. Combine the eggs, sour cream, mayonnaise and chicken broth in a large bowl. Stir to mix well. Stir in the chicken, 1/2 cup cheese, the onion, dillweed and hot sauce. Pour into the baked crust. Sprinkle with the reserved crumb mixture and top with 1/4 cup pecan halves. Bake at 325 degrees for 45 minutes.

Creamy Almond Chicken

1 tablespoon butter
$2/3$ cup sliced almonds
6 boneless skinless chicken breasts
$1/8$ teaspoon salt
$1/8$ teaspoon pepper
3 tablespoons butter
$1\frac{1}{2}$ cups heavy cream
1 tablespoon Dijon mustard
2 tablespoons orange marmalade
$1/8$ teaspoon cayenne pepper
Hot cooked rice

Melt 1 tablespoon butter in a small skillet. Add the almonds and sauté until toasted. Remove from the heat. Place the chicken breasts between 2 sheets of heavy-duty plastic wrap on a work surface. Flatten with a meat mallet or rolling pin to $1/4$ inch thick. Remove the plastic wrap and sprinkle with the salt and pepper. Melt 3 tablespoons butter in a large skillet over medium-high heat. Add the chicken and cook for 1 minute per side or until golden brown. Reduce the heat to medium. Stir in $1/2$ cup of the almonds, the cream, Dijon mustard, marmalade and cayenne pepper. Cook for 10 minutes or until the sauce thickens, stirring often. Sprinkle with the remaining almonds. Serve over hot rice.

Basil Grilled Chicken

1/4 teaspoon coarsely ground pepper
4 boneless skinless chicken breasts
5 1/3 tablespoons butter or margarine, melted
1/4 cup chopped fresh basil
1/2 cup (1 stick) butter or margarine, softened
2 tablespoons finely chopped fresh basil
1 tablespoon grated Parmesan cheese
1/4 teaspoon garlic powder
1/8 teaspoon salt
1/8 teaspoon pepper
Fresh basil sprigs

Rub 1/4 teaspoon pepper into the chicken. Mix
5 1/3 tablespoons melted butter and 1/4 cup basil in a small bowl. Brush lightly over
the chicken. Combine 1/2 cup butter, 2 tablespoons basil, the Parmesan cheese, garlic
powder, salt and 1/8 teaspoon pepper in a small bowl. Beat with an electric mixer
until fluffy. Remove to a small serving bowl. Grill the chicken over medium coals for
8 to 10 minutes per side or until the chicken is cooked through, basting often with the
remaining melted butter mixture. Discard any leftover melted butter mixture. Serve the
chicken with the basil butter and garnish with basil sprigs.

Baked Mushroom Chicken

4 (4-ounce) boneless skinless
   chicken breasts
$1/4$ cup all-purpose flour
3 tablespoons butter
1 cup sliced fresh mushrooms
$1/2$ cup chicken broth

$1/4$ teaspoon salt
$1/8$ teaspoon pepper
$1/3$ cup shredded mozzarella cheese
$1/3$ cup grated Parmesan cheese
$1/4$ cup sliced green onions

Place the chicken on a work surface. Flatten with a meat mallet or rolling pin to $1/4$ inch thick. Place the flour in a sealable plastic bag. Add the chicken a few pieces at a time and seal the bag. Shake to coat the chicken. Melt 2 tablespoons of the butter in a large skillet. Add the coated chicken and brown on both sides. Remove the chicken to a greased 7×11-inch baking dish. Add the remaining butter to the skillet. Add the mushrooms and sauté until tender. Stir in the broth, salt and pepper. Bring to a boil. Cook for 5 minutes or until the liquid is reduced to $1/2$ cup, stirring constantly. Pour evenly over the chicken. Bake at 375 degrees for 15 minutes. Sprinkle with the mozzarella cheese, Parmesan cheese and green onions. Bake for 5 minutes longer or until the chicken is cooked through.

Pecan-Crusted Chicken Breast

1/2 cup honey
2 tablespoons Dijon mustard
1 cup pecans, chopped
6 (4- to 5-ounce) boneless skinless chicken breasts

       Mix the honey and mustard in a shallow bowl. Spread the pecans in a shallow dish. Dip the chicken in the honey mixture and then coat in the pecans. Arrange in a buttered baking dish. Bake at 350 degrees for 12 to 15 minutes or until the chicken is cooked through.

Chicken Breasts with Pecan Sausage Stuffing

Serves 4

1/3 pound bulk pork sausage
5 1/3 tablespoons butter
1/3 cup finely chopped celery
1/3 cup finely chopped green
   bell pepper
1 small onion, finely chopped
1/2 cup chopped pecans
1/2 teaspoon salt
1/4 teaspoon pepper
3 cups bread crumbs

1 egg, lightly beaten
1 1/2 tablespoons milk
4 whole boneless skinless
   chicken breasts
1 1/2 tablespoons butter or
   margarine, melted
3 tablespoons fine bread crumbs
White Sauce (below)
Fresh parsley

Brown the sausage in a skillet, stirring until crumbly; drain. Melt 5 1/3 tablespoons butter in a large saucepan over medium-high heat. Add the celery, bell pepper and onion and sauté until the vegetables are tender. Add 1/3 cup of the pecans, the salt and pepper. Sauté for 3 minutes. Remove from the heat and stir in the sausage, 3 cups bread crumbs, the egg and milk. Place the chicken breasts between 2 sheets of heavy-duty plastic wrap or waxed paper on a work surface. Flatten with a meat mallet or rolling pin to 1/4 inch thick. Remove the plastic wrap and spoon the sausage mixture in the center of each chicken breast. Fold the long sides of the chicken over the stuffing and secure with a wooden pick. Place seam side down in a foil-lined baking pan. Mix 1 1/2 tablespoons butter, 3 tablespoons bread crumbs and the remaining pecans in a small bowl. Press evenly onto the chicken breasts. Bake at 350 degrees for 30 minutes or until golden brown and the chicken is cooked through. Serve with the White Sauce and garnish with chopped parsley.

White Sauce

2 tablespoons butter
2 tablespoons all-purpose flour
1/2 teaspoon salt

1/2 teaspoon white pepper
1 cup milk

Melt the butter in a saucepan. Stir in the flour, salt and pepper. Cook for 2 minutes, stirring constantly. Stir in the milk. Cook until thickened, stirring constantly.

Sesame Chicken

3 tablespoons sesame seeds
2 tablespoons all-purpose flour
1/4 teaspoon salt
1/4 teaspoon pepper
2 tablespoons soy sauce
4 (6-ounce) boneless skinless chicken breasts
1 tablespoon butter, melted

Mix the sesame seeds, flour, salt and pepper in a large sealable plastic bag. Place the soy sauce in a shallow dish. Add the chicken and turn to coat. Remove the chicken to the sesame seed mixture and discard the soy sauce. Seal the bag and shake to coat the chicken. Remove the coated chicken to a greased 9×13-inch baking dish. Drizzle with the melted butter. Bake at 400 degrees for 20 minutes or until the chicken is cooked through.

Swiss Chicken Bake

8 whole boneless skinless chicken breasts
8 slices Swiss cheese
2 (10-ounce) cans condensed cream of chicken soup
$1/4$ cup medium-dry sherry
2 cups herb-seasoned stuffing mix
$1/2$ cup (1 stick) butter, melted
Long grain and wild rice mix, cooked according to
    the package directions

Arrange the chicken in a baking pan. Top with the cheese slices. Mix the chicken soup and sherry in a bowl. Spoon evenly over the cheese. Sprinkle with the stuffing mix. Drizzle the butter over the top. Bake at 350 degrees for 40 minutes or until the chicken is cooked through. Serve over the hot rice.

*E*ntrées at cherries are delicious —
a unique experience.

*E*ntrées at Cherries
are distinctive—from the Sunday
Pork Loin with the Peach Glaze
to the Seafood Pie. For our vege-
tarian friends, we offer unique
choices, such as Spinach Pasta Pie
or Florentine Crepe Pie.

Old favorites get a
new twist, like our spicy topped
Meat Loaf or Spaghetti Pie. We
take ordinary food and make it
extraordinary at Cherries.

Entrées

CJ's Korean Beef

1 cup soy sauce
¼ cup sugar
1 cup water
1 teaspoon minced garlic
2 teaspoons chopped chives
2 teaspoons sesame seeds
3 pounds beef cubes

Mix the soy sauce, sugar, water, garlic, chives and sesame seeds in a shallow bowl or sealable plastic bag. Add the beef and turn to mix. Cover or seal the bag. Marinate in the refrigerator for 2 days before cooking to desired doneness.

Meat Loaf

1 1/2 pounds ground beef
2 onions, chopped
1 green bell pepper, chopped
1/2 cup tomato sauce
2 cups crushed saltine crackers
1 egg beaten
1 1/2 teaspoons salt
1/2 cup tomato sauce
3 tablespoons Scott's barbecue sauce
2 tablespoons light brown sugar

Combine the ground beef, onions, bell pepper, 1/2 cup tomato sauce, the crushed crackers, egg and salt in a bowl. Stir to mix well. Press into a loaf pan. Mix 1/2 cup tomato sauce, the barbecue sauce and brown sugar in a bowl. Spoon over the meat mixture. Bake at 350 degrees for 1 hour or until the meat is cooked through.

Note: This recipe was Karen's. We never dreamed it would be such a popular item.

Italian Beef and Spinach Pie

1 unbaked (9-inch) pie shell
12 ounces lean ground beef
3/4 cup chopped green bell pepper
1/2 cup sliced fresh mushrooms
1 garlic clove, minced
1 cup water
1/2 cup tomato paste
1 1/2 teaspoons Italian seasoning, crushed
1/2 teaspoon salt

1 (10-ounce) package frozen chopped
  spinach, thawed and well drained
2/3 cup ricotta cheese
1/4 cup (1 ounce) shredded
  mozzarella cheese
1 cup chopped tomato
1/2 cup (2 ounces) shredded
  mozzarella cheese

Prick the bottom and side of the pie shell with a fork. Bake at 400 degrees until light brown. Remove to a wire rack to cool. Brown the ground beef with the bell pepper, mushrooms and garlic in a skillet until the ground beef is crumbly and the vegetables are tender; drain. Stir in the water, tomato paste, Italian seasoning and salt. Bring to a boil and reduce the heat. Simmer for 10 minutes. Combine the spinach, ricotta cheese and 1/4 cup mozzarella cheese in a bowl. Stir to mix well. Spread the spinach mixture in the bottom of the baked pie shell. Top with the ground beef mixture. Bake at 350 degrees for 20 minutes. Sprinkle with the chopped tomato and 1/2 cup mozzarella cheese. Bake for 10 minutes longer. Let stand for 10 minutes before serving.

Taco Pie

1 pound ground beef
1 onion, chopped
1 (1-ounce) package taco seasoning mix
³/₄ cup water
1 (16-ounce) can pinto beans, rinsed and drained
1 (8-ounce) jar taco sauce
1 baked (9-inch) pie shell
2 cups (8 ounces) shredded Cheddar cheese
1 cup crushed corn chips
Shredded lettuce
Chopped tomato

Brown the ground beef in a skillet with the onion, stirring until the ground beef is crumbly; drain. Add the taco seasoning and water and stir to mix well. Bring to a boil and reduce the heat. Simmer for 20 minutes, stirring occasionally. Mix the pinto beans and ¹/₃ cup of the taco sauce in a bowl. Spread ¹/₂ of the bean mixture in the bottom of the pie shell. Top with ¹/₂ the meat mixture, ¹/₂ the cheese and all of the crushed corn chips. Repeat with the remaining beans, meat mixture and cheese. Bake at 400 degrees for 20 to 25 minutes. Top with shredded lettuce and chopped tomato and serve with the remaining taco sauce.

Beefy Mexican Corn Bread

1 cup yellow cornmeal
1/2 teaspoon salt
1/2 teaspoon baking soda
2 eggs, beaten
1 cup milk
1 (17-ounce) can cream-style corn
1/4 cup bacon drippings
1 tablespoon cornmeal

1 cup (4 ounces) shredded sharp
   Cheddar cheese
12 ounces ground beef, cooked
   and drained
1 onion, finely chopped
2 tablespoons chopped jalapeño chile
1 cup (4 ounces) shredded sharp
   Cheddar cheese

Mix 1 cup cornmeal, the salt and baking soda in a bowl. Add the eggs, milk, corn and bacon drippings. Stir to mix well. Sprinkle 1 tablespoon cornmeal in a well-greased cast-iron skillet. Pour 1/2 the corn bread batter into the pan. Sprinkle with 1 cup cheese. Top with the ground beef, onion and jalapeño. Top with the remaining corn bread batter and sprinkle with 1 cup cheese. Bake at 350 degrees for 40 to 50 minutes or until golden brown.

Note: Add a salad for a complete meal.

Spaghetti Pie

1/2 (12-ounce) package angel hair pasta
2 tablespoons butter or margarine
1/3 cup grated Parmesan cheese
2 eggs, well beaten
1 pound ground beef
1/2 cup chopped onion
1/4 cup chopped green bell pepper

1 (8-ounce) can stewed tomatoes
1 (6-ounce) can tomato paste
3/4 teaspoon oregano
1/2 teaspoon garlic salt
1/2 cup (2 ounces) shredded
  mozzarella cheese

Cook the pasta according to the package directions. Drain and remove to a bowl. Add the butter and Parmesan cheese to the hot pasta. Toss until the butter melts. Stir in the eggs. Spoon into a greased 10-inch pie plate, using a spoon to shape the pasta mixture into a pie shell. Bake at 350 degrees for 9 minutes or until set. Remove to a wire rack. Brown the ground beef with the onion and bell pepper in a large skillet over medium heat until the ground beef is crumbly and the vegetables are tender; drain. Stir in the stewed tomatoes, tomato paste, oregano and garlic salt. Cook, covered, for 10 minutes, stirring occasionally. Spoon over the pasta crust. Bake at 350 degrees for 15 minutes. Sprinkle with the mozzarella cheese and bake for 15 minutes longer.

Beef Stroganoff

1 pound ground beef
1 onion, chopped
2 tablespoons all-purpose flour
1/2 teaspoon garlic salt
1/4 teaspoon pepper
1 (4-ounce) can sliced mushrooms, drained
1 (10-ounce) can condensed cream of mushroom soup
1 cup sour cream
Hot cooked egg noodles
Paprika

Brown the ground beef in a skillet with the onion, stirring until the ground beef is crumbly; drain. Stir in the flour, garlic salt, pepper and mushrooms. Cook for 1 minute, stirring constantly. Stir in the mushroom soup. Simmer for 10 minutes, stirring occasionally. Stir in the sour cream and cook until heated through. Serve over noodles and sprinkle with paprika.

Note: This is Reid's favorite.

CJ's Barbecue Sauce

Makes 5 quarts

1 1/2 ounces crushed red pepper
2 tablespoons black pepper
1 tablespoon rubbed sage
1 cup sugar
3/4 cup salt
1 gallon vinegar

2 cups Scott's barbecue sauce
1/3 cup plus 1 tablespoon
   Worcestershire sauce
1/3 cup plus 1 tablespoon soy sauce
1 cup A.1. steak sauce

Mix the red pepper, black pepper, sage, sugar and salt in a large bowl. Stir in the vinegar, barbecue sauce, Worcestershire sauce, soy sauce and steak sauce. Pour into an airtight container. Store in the refrigerator for up to 3 weeks. Use to marinate any meat before cooking.

Note: C.J. is a lifelong family friend and a great cook!

CJ's Peach Glaze for Pork

Makes about 2 cups

1 teaspoon ginger
1 teaspoon salt
1/4 teaspoon pepper
1 (16-ounce) can peaches, drained
1/2 cup packed brown sugar

1/4 cup ketchup
1/4 cup cider vinegar
2 tablespoons soy sauce
1 garlic clove

Process the ginger, salt, pepper, peaches, brown sugar, ketchup, vinegar, soy sauce and garlic in a food processor until puréed. Serve over roasted pork loin.

Note: This is also good on chicken.

Sunday Pork Loin

1 (4- to 5-pound) whole boneless pork loin
1 teaspoon vegetable oil
$1/3$ cup chopped onion
$1/3$ cup chopped celery
1 garlic clove, minced
1 (10-ounce) can condensed tomato soup
$1/3$ cup water
2 tablespoons brown sugar
2 tablespoons lemon juice
2 tablespoons Worcestershire sauce
2 tablespoons Dijon mustard
$1/8$ to $1/4$ teaspoon hot red pepper sauce

Place the roast on a rack in a shallow roasting pan. Roast at 325 degrees for $1 1/2$ hours. Heat the oil in a skillet. Add the onion, celery and garlic and sauté until the vegetables are tender. Stir in the tomato soup, water, brown sugar, lemon juice, Worcestershire sauce, Dijon mustard and hot sauce. Spoon 1 cup of the tomato sauce over the pork. Roast for 45 to 55 minutes longer or until a meat thermometer inserted in the thickest part registers 160 degrees. Remove the roast to a cutting board and let stand for 10 to 15 minutes before slicing. Serve with the remaining sauce.

Oven-Cooked Country Ham

1 country ham, scrubbed, soaked in
   water overnight and drained
5 cups water

Place the ham in a large roasting pan, skin side up. Pour the water around the ham. Cover tightly with foil or a lid. Place in a cold oven and set the temperature to 500 degrees. Bake for 20 minutes. Turn off the oven and leave the ham in the oven for 3 hours. Set the oven temperature to 500 degrees and bake the ham for 15 minutes. Turn off the oven and leave the ham in the oven overnight; do not open the oven door.

CJ's Stuffed Banana Peppers

Serves 6

1 pound bulk hot pork sausage
1 pound sweet banana peppers
1/4 cup olive oil
15 Roma tomatoes, halved
2 garlic cloves, minced
1 tablespoon chopped fresh oregano
2 tablespoons chopped fresh basil
16 ounces angel hair pasta, cooked al dente and drained

Brown the sausage in a skillet, stirring until crumbly; drain. Cut the tops off the peppers and remove the seeds. Stuff the pepper cavities with the cooked sausage. Heat the olive oil in a skillet. Add the tomato halves and sauté lightly. Stir in the garlic, oregano and basil. Cook for 15 minutes or until heated through. Spread the pasta in a 9×13-inch baking dish or individual ramekins. Top with the tomato mixture. Place the peppers on the tomatoes. Bake at 350 degrees for 20 minutes or until the peppers are tender-crisp.

Note: Be sure to use sweet banana peppers, not hot peppers!

Crispy Baked Tilapia

1 cup sour cream
2 tablespoons finely chopped onion
1 tablespoon Worcestershire sauce
1 sleeve saltine crackers, crushed
Paprika
6 (5- to 7-ounce) tilapia fillets

         Mix the sour cream, onion and Worcestershire sauce together in a shallow bowl. Mix the crushed crackers and paprika together in a shallow dish. Coat the fish in the sour cream mixture and then press into the crushed crackers to coat. Arrange in a buttered baking dish. Bake at 350 degrees for 20 to 25 minutes or until the fish flakes easily.

crab cakes

1 pound fresh lump or back-fin crab meat, drained and flaked
1 egg, lightly beaten
1 tablespoon mayonnaise
1/2 cup crushed cornflakes
3 tablespoons chopped fresh parsley
1 1/2 tablespoons Old Bay seasoning
Freshly ground pepper
1/4 cup (1/2 stick) butter

Combine the crab meat, egg, mayonnaise, cornflakes, parsley, Old Bay seasoning and pepper in a large bowl. Stir gently to mix. Shape into 6 patties and place on a plate. Cover and chill for 1 hour. Melt the butter in a large heavy skillet. Add the crab cakes and brown on both sides.

Crab Imperial

1 pound back-fin crab meat, flaked
1 egg, beaten
3/4 cup mayonnaise
1 teaspoon Old Bay seasoning
Juice of 1/2 lemon
1 1/2 teaspoons Worcestershire sauce
1/4 teaspoon hot red pepper sauce (or to taste)

Mix the crab meat and egg in a large bowl. Combine the mayonnaise, Old Bay seasoning, lemon juice, Worcestershire sauce and hot sauce in a bowl. Stir to mix well. Add to the crab meat mixture and stir to mix well. Spoon into buttered clean oyster shells and place on a baking sheet. Bake at 375 degrees for 10 to 15 minutes or until firm and light brown. Serve immediately.

crab quiche

2 eggs, beaten
1/2 cup mayonnaise
2 tablespoons all-purpose flour
1 teaspoon Old Bay seasoning
1/2 cup milk
1 (6-ounce) package frozen crab meat, thawed, drained and flaked
2 cups (8 ounces) shredded Swiss cheese
1/3 cup chopped green onions
1 (1-crust) pie pastry

Combine the eggs, mayonnaise, flour, Old Bay seasoning and milk in a bowl. Stir to mix well. Stir in the crab meat, cheese and green onions. Fit the pastry into a quiche dish. Spoon the crab mixture into the quiche shell. Bake at 350 degrees until set.

Seafood Medley

3/4 cup (1 1/2 sticks) butter
3/4 cup all-purpose flour
3 cups half-and-half
1 1/2 teaspoons salt
1/2 teaspoon cayenne pepper
1 tablespoon onion juice
1 pound claw crab meat
1 pound scallops, steamed 2 minutes in their own juice
1 pound cooked shrimp, peeled
1 pound orange roughy, baked until the fish flakes easily
1/2 cup (2 ounces) bread crumbs

Melt the butter in a large saucepan. Stir in the flour. Cook for 2 minutes, stirring constantly. Stir in the half-and-half, salt and cayenne pepper. Cook until thick, stirring constantly. Stir in the onion juice, crab meat, scallops, shrimp and orange roughy. Spoon into a buttered 9×13-inch baking dish. Sprinkle with the bread crumbs. Bake at 325 degrees for 20 minutes or until bubbly.

Seafood Pie

2 1/2 cups crushed potato chips
2 tablespoons butter, melted
1 egg
8 ounces cooked shrimp, peeled
Imitation crab meat
Chopped celery
Chopped red or green bell pepper
Finely chopped onion
Mayonnaise
Old Bay seasoning
Cayenne pepper
1/2 cup (2 ounces) shredded Cheddar

cheese

Mix the crushed potato chips, melted butter and egg in a bowl. Press onto the bottom and up the side of 9-inch pie plate. Bake at 375 degrees for 5 minutes. Remove to a wire rack to cool. Mix the shrimp, crab meat, celery, bell pepper, onion, mayonnaise, Old Bay seasoning and cayenne pepper in a bowl. Spoon into the baked crust. Sprinkle with the cheese. Bake at 375 degrees for 20 to 25 minutes or until the cheese melts.

Cashew Shrimp

1/2 cup chicken broth
1 tablespoon cornstarch
1 tablespoon soy sauce
1/4 teaspoon pepper
2 tablespoons peanut or vegetable oil
1 pound fresh deveined peeled shrimp
1 tablespoon soy sauce
1 1/2 cups julienned red bell peppers
1 teaspoon minced garlic
1 (8-ounce) can sliced water chestnuts, drained
1 (6-ounce) package frozen snow peas, thawed and drained
Hot cooked rice
1/2 cup toasted cashews
1/4 cup chopped scallions

Combine the broth, cornstarch, 1 tablespoon soy sauce and the pepper in a small bowl. Stir to dissolve the cornstarch and set aside. Heat the oil in a wok or large nonstick skillet. Add the shrimp and 1 tablespoon soy sauce and stir-fry until the shrimp turn pink. Remove the shrimp with a slotted spoon to a plate. Add the bell peppers and garlic to the wok and stir-fry for 1 minute. Add the water chestnuts and snow peas and stir-fry until heated through. Add the cornstarch mixture and cooked shrimp. Cook until thick and bubbly, stirring constantly. Serve over hot rice and top with the cashews and scallions.

Shrimp and Angel Hair Casserole

1 tablespoon butter, softened
2 eggs, beaten
1 cup half-and-half
1 cup plain yogurt
1/3 cup crumbled feta cheese
1/2 cup (2 ounces) shredded Swiss cheese
2 tablespoons chopped fresh parsley
1 teaspoon basil
1 teaspoon oregano
1 package angel hair pasta, cooked al dente and drained
1 pound lightly cooked medium shrimp, peeled
1/2 cup (2 ounces) shredded Monterey Jack cheese

Grease a baking dish with the butter. Combine the eggs, half-and-half, yogurt, feta cheese, Swiss cheese, parsley, basil and oregano in a bowl. Stir to mix well. Pour into the prepared baking dish. Add the pasta and stir to mix well. Top with the shrimp and sprinkle with the Monterey Jack cheese. Bake at 350 degrees for 20 minutes or until bubbly and the shrimp turn pink.

Spinach Pasta Pie

1/2 (12-ounce) package angel hair pasta

2 tablespoons butter, softened

1/3 cup grated Parmesan cheese

2 eggs, beaten

1 (10-ounce) package frozen chopped spinach, thawed,
    drained and squeezed dry

3 eggs, beaten

1 cup (4 ounces) shredded mozzarella cheese

1/3 cup milk

1/2 teaspoon salt

1/4 teaspoon freshly ground pepper

1/4 teaspoon onion powder

1/8 teaspoon nutmeg

Cook the pasta according to the package directions. Drain and remove to a bowl. Add the butter and Parmesan cheese to the hot pasta. Toss until the butter melts. Stir in 2 eggs. Spoon into a lightly greased 9-inch pie plate, using a spoon to shape the pasta mixture into a pie shell. Cover with foil. Bake at 350 degrees for 10 minutes. Remove to a wire rack and remove the foil. Mix the spinach, 3 eggs, the mozzarella cheese, milk, salt, pepper, onion powder and nutmeg in a bowl. Spoon into the pasta shell. Bake at 350 degrees for 25 to 30 minutes or until hot. Let stand for 10 minutes before slicing.

Spinach Lasagna

16 ounces ricotta cheese

1 egg

1/4 cup chopped onion

1 cup (4 ounces) shredded mozzarella cheese

1/4 cup (1 ounce) grated Parmesan cheese

2 (16-ounce) packages frozen chopped spinach,
    thawed and drained

1 teaspoon basil

1/2 teaspoon garlic powder

1 (16-ounce) package lasagna noodles, cooked al dente and drained

Favorite marinara sauce

1 cup (4 ounces) shredded mozzarella cheese

Combine the ricotta cheese, egg, onion, 1 cup mozzarella cheese, the Parmesan cheese, spinach, basil and garlic powder in a large bowl. Stir to mix well. Lay the noodles on a work surface. Top each with the spinach mixture and roll up. Cover the bottom of 6 individual baking dishes with marinara sauce. Place 1 lasagna roll in each dish. Pour marinara sauce over the lasagna rolls and sprinkle 1 cup mozzarella cheese over the tops. Bake at 350 degrees for 15 minutes or until heated through.

Florentine Crepe Pie

1 (10-ounce) package frozen chopped
   spinach, cooked and well drained
1/4 cup Swiss Cheese Sauce (below)
1 tablespoon butter or
   margarine, melted
1 cup chopped fresh mushrooms
2 tablespoons finely chopped
   green onions

8 ounces cream cheese, softened
1 egg, beaten
1/2 cup Swiss Cheese Sauce (below)
1 recipe Crepes (page 28)
1/4 cup (1 ounce) shredded Swiss cheese
1 teaspoon paprika

Combine the spinach and 1/4 cup Swiss Cheese Sauce in a
bowl. Stir to mix well. Melt the butter in a skillet. Add the mushrooms and green onions
and sauté until the vegetables are tender. Combine the cream cheese and egg in a bowl.
Beat with an electric mixer at medium speed until smooth. Add the mushroom mixture
and 1/2 cup Swiss Cheese Sauce. Stir to mix well. Place 1 crepe in a lightly greased
10-inch quiche dish or pie plate. Spread about 2 tablespoons of the spinach mixture
over the crepe. Top with another crepe. Spread about 2 tablespoons of the mushroom
mixture over the crepe. Repeat the layers to use the remaining crepes, spinach mixture
and mushroom mixture, ending with a crepe on top. Sprinkle with 1/4 cup Swiss cheese
and the paprika. Bake at 375 degrees for 25 minutes or until the sauce is bubbly and the
top is lightly browned.

Swiss Cheese Sauce

1/4 cup (1/2 stick) butter or margarine
1/3 cup all-purpose flour
2 3/4 cups milk
1/2 teaspoon salt
1/8 teaspoon pepper

1/4 teaspoon nutmeg
1/4 cup heavy cream
1 cup (4 ounces) shredded Swiss cheese
2 tablespoons grated Parmesan cheese

Melt the butter in a heavy saucepan over low heat. Stir in
the flour until smooth. Cook for 1 minute, stirring constantly. Stir in the milk gradually.
Cook over medium heat until thickened, stirring constantly. Stir in the salt, pepper,
nutmeg and cream. Add the Swiss cheese and Parmesan cheese. Cook until the cheeses
melt, stirring constantly.

Creamy Spinach Crepes

2 (10-ounce) packages frozen chopped spinach, thawed,
    drained and squeezed dry
2 cups milk
3 tablespoons butter
1/4 cup all-purpose flour
1 chicken bouillon cube, crushed
1 teaspoon salt
1/4 teaspoon pepper
1/2 teaspoon garlic powder
1 recipe Crepes (page 28)
1/2 cup (2 ounces) shredded Swiss cheese

Purée the spinach and milk in a blender. Melt the butter in a skillet. Stir in the flour until smooth. Stir in the bouillon cube, salt, pepper and garlic powder. Cook until hot and smooth, stirring constantly. Stir in the spinach mixture. Cook until thick, stirring constantly. Lay the crepes on a work surface. Spoon 1/3 cup of the spinach mixture over each crepe. Roll up and place in a buttered baking dish. Bake at 375 degrees for 15 minutes. Sprinkle with the cheese and bake for 5 minutes longer.

Fettuccine Alfredo

¹/4 cup (¹/2 stick) butter
1 cup heavy cream
2 eggs, beaten
¹/2 cup (2 ounces) grated Parmesan cheese
2 teaspoons minced garlic
2 tablespoons chopped fresh parsley
8 ounces fettuccini, cooked al dente and drained

Melt the butter in a saucepan. Stir in the cream. Whisk the eggs and cheese in a bowl. Stir into the cream mixture gradually. Add the garlic and parsley. Cook until thickened, stirring constantly. Serve over the hot pasta.

Sides at cherries are outstanding—
the perfect accompaniment.

Sides at Cherries
add a different edge to your
everyday fare. Hearty soups
complement our crisp salads
or our unique collection of
sandwiches. Our customers really love the Special Sandwich,
with its unusual combination of
turkey and apples.

The Vidalia Deep
Dish makes a pork chop special.
The season's freshest tomatoes
make the Marinated Tomatoes
perfect for summer entertaining.
Sides complete the meal at
Cherries.

Sides

chicken chili

2 tablespoons vegetable oil

3 cups coarsely chopped boneless skinless chicken breasts

1 cup chopped onion

1 green bell pepper, chopped

2 garlic cloves, minced

2 (14-ounce) cans stewed tomatoes

1 (16-ounce) can pinto beans, drained and rinsed

3/4 cup picante sauce

1 teaspoon chili powder

1 teaspoon cumin

1/2 teaspoon salt

Heat the oil in a skillet. Add the chicken and sauté until light brown. Add the onion, bell pepper and garlic and sauté until the vegetables are tender. Remove to a large saucepan. Stir in the stewed tomatoes, beans, picante sauce, chili powder, cumin and salt. Simmer over medium heat for 30 minutes.

Seafood Stew

1/4 cup olive oil
1 1/2 cups chopped onions
2 tablespoons chopped garlic
4 teaspoons oregano
2 1/2 cups crushed tomatoes
2 1/2 cups bottled clam juice
1 cup dry white wine
2 (6-ounce) cans chopped clams, drained and
    liquid reserved
1 pound fresh large deveined peeled shrimp
1 (6-ounce) can crab meat, drained and flaked
1/2 cup chopped fresh basil
Salt to taste
Black pepper to taste
Cayenne pepper to taste

Heat the olive oil in a large heavy saucepan over medium heat. Add the onions, garlic and oregano and sauté for 10 minutes or until the vegetables are tender. Stir in the tomatoes, clam juice, wine and reserved clam liquid. Increase the heat and bring to a boil. Boil for 15 minutes or until slightly thickened. Stir in the clams, shrimp and crab meat. Reduce the heat and simmer for 2 minutes. Stir in the basil. Simmer until the shrimp turn pink. Season with salt, black pepper and cayenne pepper.

Crab Bisque

1 (10-ounce) can condensed cream of mushroom soup
1 (10-ounce) can condensed cream of asparagus soup
2 cups milk
1 cup light cream
1 (7-ounce) can crab meat
1/4 cup white wine

Mix the mushroom soup and asparagus soup in a saucepan. Stir in the milk and cream. Heat to boiling, stirring occasionally. Stir in the crab meat. Cook until heated through. Stir in the wine just before serving.

crab and corn chowder

¹/4 cup (¹/2 stick) butter
2 onions, chopped
1 cup chopped celery
¹/3 cup all-purpose flour
2 cups milk
4 cups cubed red-skinned potatoes
3 garlic cloves, minced
12 ears fresh corn
2 cups milk
1¹/2 tablespoons Old Bay seasoning
Salt and pepper to taste
1 pound fresh lump or back-fin crab meat

Melt the butter in a saucepan. Add the onions and celery and sauté until the onions are light brown. Stir in the flour. Cook for 2 minutes, stirring constantly. Stir in 2 cups milk. Cook until thickened, stirring constantly. Remove from the heat. Boil the potatoes and garlic in a large saucepan with enough water to cover just until the potatoes are tender. Cut the kernels from the corn and add to the boiling potatoes. Cook for 10 minutes, adding more water, if necessary. Stir in the white sauce, 2 cups milk and the Old Bay seasoning. Season with salt and pepper. Bring back to a boil and reduce the heat. Simmer for 10 minutes or until the soup thickens, stirring often. Stir in the crab meat just before serving.

clam chowder

1/3 pound bacon slices, diced
3 onions, chopped
3 tablespoons all-purpose flour
2 large cans chopped clams, drained and liquid reserved
5 large potatoes, diced
1 tablespoon salt
1/4 teaspoon celery salt
1/4 teaspoon pepper
5 cups milk
2 tablespoons butter

Cook the bacon in a large saucepan until light brown. Add the onions and sauté until tender. Stir in the flour. Cook for 2 minutes, stirring constantly. Add enough water to the reserved clam liquid to measure 2 cups. Stir into the onion mixture. Cook until slightly thickened, stirring constantly. Stir in the potatoes, salt, celery salt and pepper. Cook, covered, for 10 minutes or until the potatoes are tender. Stir in the milk, butter and clams. Cook, covered, for 5 minutes or until heated through, stirring occasionally.

Turkey Corn Chowder

Serves 10 to 12

¹/₄ cup (¹/₂ stick) butter
4 onions, sliced
5 potatoes, cubed
2 ribs celery, chopped
1 tablespoon salt
2 cups chicken broth
5 cups milk
2 (15-ounce) cans whole kernel corn, drained, or
   3¹/₂ cups frozen corn kernels
1 (14-ounce) can cream-style corn
1 cup half-and-half
1¹/₂ teaspoons paprika
¹/₄ teaspoon thyme
3 cups chopped cooked turkey

Melt the butter in a large saucepan. Add the onions and sauté until tender. Stir in the potatoes, celery, salt, broth, milk and whole kernel corn. Bring to a boil and reduce the heat. Simmer, covered, for 15 minutes or until the vegetables are tender. Stir in the cream-style corn, half-and-half, paprika, thyme and turkey. Cook until heated through. Garnish with chopped parsley and serve.

Taco Soup

2 pounds ground beef
1 small onion, chopped
1 (1-ounce) package taco seasoning mix
1 (1-ounce) package ranch salad dressing mix
1½ cups water
1 (16-ounce) can pinto beans
1 (15-ounce) can lima beans
1 (15-ounce) can hominy
2 (14-ounce) cans stewed tomatoes
1 (10-ounce) can tomatoes with green chiles
1 teaspoon salt
1 teaspoon pepper

Brown the ground beef in a large saucepan with the onion, stirring until the ground beef is crumbly; drain. Stir in the taco seasoning mix, salad dressing mix and water. Stir in the pinto beans, lima beans, hominy, stewed tomatoes, tomatoes with green chiles, salt and pepper. Simmer for 30 minutes.

Ham and Swiss Soup

1½ tablespoons butter
1½ tablespoons all-purpose flour
1 (14-ounce) can reduced-sodium chicken broth
1 cup chopped broccoli
2 tablespoons chopped onion
1 cup chopped ham
½ cup heavy cream
⅛ teaspoon thyme
¾ cup (3 ounces) shredded Swiss cheese

Melt the butter in a saucepan. Whisk in the flour until smooth. Cook for 2 minutes, whisking constantly. Stir in the broth gradually. Bring to a boil. Cook for 2 minutes or until thickened, stirring constantly. Stir in the broccoli and onion. Cook until the vegetables are tender-crisp. Stir in the ham, cream and thyme. Cook until heated through. Add the cheese and cook until the cheese melts, stirring often.

Southwestern Chicken Soup

Serves 6 to 8

1 to 2 tablespoons canola oil or vegetable oil
1 1/4 pounds boneless skinless chicken breasts,
    cut into thin strips
2 (14-ounce) cans chicken broth
1 (16-ounce) package frozen corn kernels
1 (14-ounce) can diced tomatoes
1 onion, chopped
1 green bell pepper, chopped
1 red bell pepper, chopped
1 (4-ounce) can chopped green chiles
1 teaspoon cumin
1/2 teaspoon garlic powder
1 1/2 teaspoons seasoned salt (optional)

Heat the canola oil in a large skillet. Add the chicken and sauté until light brown. Remove to a large saucepan. Stir in the broth, corn, tomatoes, onion, green bell pepper, red bell pepper, green chiles, cumin, garlic powder and seasoned salt. Bring to a boil and reduce the heat to low. Simmer until the onion and bell peppers are tender.

Italian Chicken Rice Soup

1 (49-ounce) can chicken broth
1 (26-ounce) jar meatless spaghetti sauce
1 1/2 cups cubed cooked chicken
2 tablespoons finely chopped fresh parsley
1/2 to 1 teaspoon thyme
3 cups cooked rice
1 teaspoon sugar

Mix the broth, spaghetti sauce, chicken, parsley and thyme in a soup kettle or Dutch oven. Bring to a boil and reduce the heat. Simmer, uncovered, for 10 minutes. Stir in the rice and sugar. Simmer, uncovered, for 10 minutes longer or until heated through.

Tomato and Fresh Basil Soup

Serves 10 to 12

3 tablespoons olive oil
2 tablespoons butter
2 onions, chopped
1/4 cup all-purpose flour
3 cups chicken broth
1/4 cup chopped fresh basil
1/4 cup chopped fresh parsley
2 (26-ounce) cans chopped tomatoes
1 (6-ounce) can tomato paste
1 tablespoon sugar
1 teaspoon pepper

Heat the olive oil and butter in a large saucepan. Add the onions and sauté until tender. Stir in the flour. Cook for 2 minutes, stirring constantly. Stir in the broth gradually. Stir in the basil and parsley. Bring to a boil. Cook for 10 minutes or until slightly thickened, stirring often. Stir in the tomatoes, tomato paste, sugar and pepper. Bring to a boil and reduce the heat. Simmer for 30 minutes.

French Onion Soup au Gratin

2 tablespoons butter or margarine
2 onions, very thinly sliced
4 cups beef broth
$1/2$ cup water
Salt and pepper to taste

$1/2$ cup madeira (optional)
Parmesan Croutons (below)
$1/2$ cup (2 ounces) shredded
   Swiss cheese

Melt the butter in a large skillet. Stir in the onions. Cook, covered, for 5 minutes or until tender. Cook, uncovered, until the onions are well browned, stirring occasionally. Stir in the broth and water. Simmer, covered, for 30 minutes. Season with salt and pepper and stir in the madeira. Ladle into 8 ovenproof soup bowls. Float a Parmesan Crouton on top of each and sprinkle with the cheese. Place the bowls in a shallow baking pan. Bake at 400 degrees for 15 minutes or until the cheese is melted and golden brown.

Parmesan Croutons

4 (1-inch) slices French bread, cut in half
$1/4$ cup ($1/2$ stick) butter or margarine, melted
$1/4$ cup (1 ounce) grated Parmesan cheese

Brush both sides of the bread with the melted butter. Arrange the bread on a baking sheet and sprinkle the cheese on top. Bake at 350 degrees for 20 minutes or until golden brown and crisp.

chinese slaw

Serves 6

1 package sliced almonds
2 tablespoons sesame seeds
1 (3-ounce) package chicken-flavor ramen noodles
1/2 bag coleslaw mix or 1/2 head cabbage, shredded
4 green onions, chopped
2 chicken breasts, cooked and chopped
1/2 cup vegetable oil
3 tablespoons vinegar
2 tablespoons sugar
1 tablespoon salt
1 teaspoon pepper

Spread the almonds and sesame seeds on a baking sheet. Toast at 350 degrees for 5 minutes, stirring once. Remove to a plate to cool. Break up the ramen noodles into a large bowl. Add the coleslaw, green onions, chicken, almonds and sesame seeds. Toss to mix. Whisk the seasoning packet from the ramen noodles, oil, vinegar, sugar, salt and pepper in a bowl. Add to the cabbage mixture and toss to coat. Chill for 4 hours before serving.

Crunchy Romaine Toss

1/4 cup (1/2 stick) unsalted butter
1 (3-ounce) package ramen noodles
1 cup walnuts, chopped
1 bunch broccoli, coarsely chopped

1 head romaine lettuce, rinsed, dried
   and torn into bite-size pieces
4 green onions, chopped
1 cup Sweet-and-Sour Dressing (below)

Melt the butter in a skillet. Discard the seasoning packet from the ramen noodles and break up the noodles. Add the ramen noodles and walnuts to the skillet. Sauté until golden brown. Remove to paper towels to drain. Combine the broccoli, romaine, green onions, walnuts and noodles in a large bowl. Toss to mix. Add the Sweet-and-Sour Dressing and toss to coat.

Sweet-and-Sour Dressing

1 cup vegetable oil
1 cup sugar
1/2 cup red wine vinegar

1 tablespoon soy sauce
Salt and pepper to taste

Whisk the oil, sugar, vinegar and soy sauce in a bowl. Season with salt and pepper.

spinach and Strawberry Salad

2 cups torn washed spinach
2 cups torn washed leaf lettuce
1 cup sliced fresh strawberries
3 hard-cooked eggs, sliced

1 small red onion, sliced
1/2 cup sliced almonds, toasted
Strawberry Vinaigrette (below)

Combine the spinach, lettuce, strawberries, eggs, onion and almonds in a large bowl. Toss to mix. Add the Strawberry Vinaigrette and toss to coat.

Strawberry Vinaigrette

1/3 cup strawberry jam
1/3 cup red wine vinegar
1 cup vegetable oil
1 tablespoon poppy seeds

Whisk the jam, vinegar, oil and poppy seeds in a bowl.

Frozen Strawberry Salad

8 ounces cream cheese, softened
$^3/_4$ cup sugar
1 (10-ounce) package frozen sliced strawberries, thawed
1 (20-ounce) can pineapple tidbits, drained
$^1/_2$ cup pecans, chopped
1 (16-ounce) container frozen whipped topping, thawed

Beat the cream cheese and sugar in a large bowl until light and fluffy. Fold in the strawberries, pineapple, pecans and whipped topping. Spoon into a 9×11-inch baking dish. Cover and freeze until firm.

Crunchy Reuben Sandwich

1 egg
1/4 cup milk
1 bag corn chips, crushed
12 to 14 slices rye bread
Dijon mustard
1 pound shaved corned beef
1/3 pound Swiss cheese, sliced
1 can sauerkraut, drained

Beat the egg and milk in shallow bowl. Spread the crushed corn chips in a shallow dish. Dip 1 side of each bread slice into the egg mixture and then coat in the corn chips. Spread the uncoated side of the bread with mustard. Arrange 1/2 the slices, coated side down, on a baking sheet. Top with the corned beef, cheese and sauerkraut. Place the remaining bread slices on top, coated side up. Bake at 350 degrees for 10 to 12 minutes or until the cheese melts.

caríbbean chícken Crescent Sandwíches

1 pound boneless chicken,
   cut into 1/2-inch pieces
1 teaspoon seasoned salt
1/2 teaspoon garlic powder
1/4 teaspoon cayenne pepper (optional)
4 to 6 tablespoons butter or margarine
6 ounces cream cheese

1/4 cup spicy or regular mango chutney
1/2 cup chopped green bell pepper
1/2 cup sliced green onions
3 (8-count) cans refrigerator
   crescent rolls
1 egg white, lightly beaten
1/2 teaspoon sesame seeds

Sprinkle the chicken with the seasoned salt, garlic powder and cayenne pepper. Melt the butter in a large skillet. Add the chicken and sauté until the chicken is cooked through. Add the cream cheese and chutney. Cook until the cream cheese melts, stirring constantly. Remove from the heat and stir in the bell pepper and green onions. Unroll the crescent dough on a work surface. Press the seams between 2 rolls to seal to make 12 rectangles. Arrange on an ungreased baking sheet. Spoon 1/4 cup of the chicken mixture on 1/2 of each rectangle. Fold the dough over the chicken mixture and press the edges with a fork to seal. Brush the tops with the egg white and sprinkle with the sesame seeds. Bake at 375 degrees for 15 to 20 minutes.

Note: Joy Beshears shared this great recipe with us.

Open-Face Chicken Sandwich

2 tablespoons butter
10 (4-ounce) boneless chicken breasts
1 teaspoon salt
1 1/2 cups mayonnaise
1/2 cup sliced green onions
1 teaspoon dillweed, crushed
5 English muffins, split and toasted
1 (20-ounce) can sliced pineapple, drained
1 1/2 cups (6 ounces) shredded Cheddar cheese

Melt the butter in a skillet. Add the chicken and sauté until golden brown and cooked through. Remove from the heat and sprinkle with the salt. Mix the mayonnaise, green onions and dillweed in a bowl. Spread 1/2 the mayonnaise mixture on the muffin halves. Top each with 1 chicken breast. Place 1 pineapple slice on top of the chicken. Spread with the remaining mayonnaise mixture and sprinkle with the cheese. Arrange on a baking sheet. Bake at 350 degrees until the cheese is bubbly and browned.

Mushroom Crab Melt

3 slices bacon, diced
1 cup sliced fresh mushrooms
1/4 cup chopped onion
1 (6-ounce) can crab meat, drained and flaked
1 cup (4 ounces) shredded Swiss cheese
1/2 cup mayonnaise
1/3 cup grated Parmesan cheese
2 tablespoons butter or margarine, softened
6 English muffins, split
Dash of cayenne pepper
Dash of paprika

Cook the bacon in a skillet over medium heat until crisp. Remove to paper towels to drain; crumble. Remove all but 2 tablespoons of bacon drippings from the skillet. Add the mushrooms and onion. Sauté until the vegetables are tender. Combine the crab meat, Swiss cheese, mayonnaise, Parmesan cheese, mushroom mixture and bacon in a large bowl. Stir to mix well. Spread the butter on the muffin halves. Top with the crab meat mixture. Sprinkle with the cayenne pepper and paprika. Arrange on a baking sheet. Bake at 400 degrees for 10 to 15 minutes or until light brown.

Note: You may use 1 cup chopped imitation crab meat instead of the canned crab meat.

special sandwich

3 Granny Smith apples
Lemon juice
1 loaf cinnamon raisin bread
3 ounces cream cheese, softened
1 pound sliced cooked turkey breast
8 ounces sliced Swiss cheese
Alfalfa sprouts

Core and slice the apples. Dip the apple slices in lemon juice to prevent browning. Spread the bread slices with the cream cheese. Top 1/2 the bread slices with the turkey, Swiss cheese, apples and sprouts. Top with the remaining bread slices.

Note: This is a cool refreshing sandwich. Serve with fresh fruit or a pasta salad.

Fresh Vegetable Sandwich

Serves 8

1 1/2 teaspoons unflavored gelatin
2 tablespoons cold water
2 tablespoons boiling water
2 cups mayonnaise
1 teaspoon salt
1/4 teaspoon Tabasco sauce
1 tablespoon lemon juice
1 green bell pepper, chopped
1 cucumber, chopped
2 tomatoes, chopped
1 red onion, finely chopped
1 cup finely chopped celery

Dissolve the gelatin in the cold water in a small bowl. Stir in the boiling water. Remove to a large bowl and let cool. Add the mayonnaise, salt, Tabasco sauce and lemon juice. Stir to mix well. Add the bell pepper, cucumber, tomatoes, onion and celery. Stir to mix well. Pour into a 5×9-inch loaf dish. Cover and chill for 2 hours or until set. Unmold onto a work surface and slice. Use as a sandwich or salad.

Broccoli Casserole

2 (10-ounce) packages frozen broccoli spears
1 (10-ounce) can condensed cream of celery soup
1 egg, beaten
1/2 cup mayonnaise
1 onion, grated
1/2 teaspoon salt
1/4 teaspoon pepper
1 cup (4 ounces) shredded Cheddar cheese
1 sleeve butter crackers, crushed

Arrange the broccoli in a greased baking dish. Combine the soup, egg, mayonnaise, onion, salt and pepper in a bowl. Stir to mix well. Pour over the broccoli. Top with the cheese and sprinkle with the crackers. Bake, covered, at 325 degrees for 30 minutes. Uncover and bake for 10 minutes longer.

Vidalia Deep Dish

2 cups water
1 cup long grain rice
1/2 cup (1 stick) butter or margarine
6 large Vidalia onions, chopped
1 cup (4 ounces) shredded Swiss cheese
1 cup heavy cream
2 tablespoons chopped fresh parsley
1/4 teaspoon salt
1/4 teaspoon white pepper
Paprika

Bring the water to a boil in a saucepan. Stir in the rice and reduce the heat. Simmer, covered, for 10 minutes or until the water is absorbed. Remove from the heat. Melt the butter in a Dutch oven over medium heat. Add the onions and sauté for 15 minutes. Remove from the heat. Stir in the rice, cheese, cream, parsley, salt and white pepper. Spoon into a lightly greased 9×13-inch baking dish. Bake, covered, at 350 degrees for 30 minutes. Sprinkle with paprika.

Pineapple Casserole

3 eggs
1/2 cup sugar
1 (20-ounce) can crushed pineapple
1/4 teaspoon salt
2 or 3 slices bread, torn into pieces
1/2 cup (1 stick) butter, melted

Beat the eggs in a bowl. Stir in the sugar, undrained pineapple and salt. Pour into a shallow casserole. Top with the bread. Drizzle the melted butter evenly over the bread. Bake at 350 degrees for 20 to 25 minutes or until set.

Note: Pineapple Casserole is excellent with ham or pork.

Greenbriers Potatoes

5 pounds potatoes, peeled,
  thinly sliced and rinsed
2 cups heavy cream
2 garlic cloves, minced
$1/2$ teaspoon salt
$1/2$ teaspoon pepper
$2^{3}/4$ cups (11 ounces) shredded Parmesan cheese
6 eggs, lightly beaten
$3/4$ cup (3 ounces) shredded Parmesan cheese

Combine the potatoes, cream, garlic, salt and pepper in a large saucepan. Bring to a boil and reduce the heat. Simmer, covered, for 30 minutes or until the potatoes are tender-crisp. Remove from the heat and stir in $2^{3}/4$ cups cheese. Stir in the eggs gradually. Pour into a greased 9×13-inch baking pan. Sprinkle with $3/4$ cup cheese. Bake at 400 degrees for 20 to 25 minutes or until the potatoes are tender.

Squash and Potato Casserole

4 yellow squash, sliced
4 potatoes, peeled and sliced
1 onion, sliced
1/2 cup (1 stick) butter, cut into pieces
Salt and pepper to taste
1 cup sour cream
1 1/2 cups (6 ounces) shredded Cheddar cheese

Arrange 1/2 of the squash, 1/2 of the potatoes and 1/2 of the onions in a buttered 9×13-inch casserole dish. Dot with 1/2 of the butter and season with salt and pepper. Repeat the layers to use the remaining squash, potatoes, onion and butter. Season with salt and pepper. Cover with foil. Bake at 300 degrees for 2 hours. Uncover and spread the sour cream over the top. Sprinkle with the cheese. Bake, uncovered, for 30 minutes longer or until the vegetables are tender.

Note: Betty Hicks served this to Ollie at a bridge luncheon. It is wonderful!

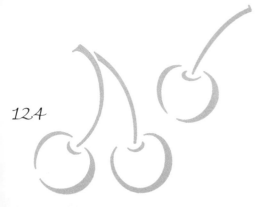

Squash with white Cheddar cheese

Serves 6

1 cup sliced onion (about 1 onion)
2 pounds yellow summer squash, chopped
$1/2$ teaspoon salt
Freshly ground pepper to taste
2 eggs
2 tablespoons sugar
$1/2$ cup milk
2 cups (8 ounces) shredded white Cheddar cheese
1 to 2 tablespoons butter, thinly sliced

Cook the onion and squash in a small amount of boiling water in a saucepan for 3 minutes or until almost tender; drain well. Arrange the onion and squash in a 2-quart baking dish. Sprinkle with the salt and season with pepper. Beat the eggs, sugar and milk in a bowl. Stir in the cheese. Pour over the squash mixture. Dot with the butter. Bake for 35 to 45 minutes or until set.

Marinated Tomatoes

1/3 cup olive oil
1/4 cup red wine vinegar
2 teaspoons dried parsley flakes
1 teaspoon finely chopped onion
1 teaspoon Italian seasoning

1/2 teaspoon sugar
1/4 teaspoon garlic salt
1/4 teaspoon pepper
4 large tomatoes, sliced

Whisk the olive oil, vinegar, parsley flakes, onion, Italian seasoning, sugar, garlic salt and pepper in a bowl. Pour over the tomatoes in a shallow dish. Cover and chill for 2 hours.

Zucchini and Tomato Casserole

1/4 cup vegetable oil
1 garlic clove, minced
4 zucchini, sliced
1 tablespoon chopped fresh oregano
1 tablespoon chopped fresh basil
1/2 cup (2 ounces) shredded
    Cheddar cheese

1/4 cup (1 ounce) grated
    Parmesan cheese
4 tomatoes, peeled and sliced
Salt and pepper to taste
1/2 cup bread crumbs
3 tablespoons butter, melted

Heat the oil in a skillet. Add the garlic and zucchini and sauté until lightly cooked. Stir in the oregano and basil and remove from the heat. Mix the Cheddar cheese and Parmesan cheese together in a bowl. Alternate layers of zucchini, tomatoes and the cheese mixture in a buttered 9×11-inch baking dish, seasoning each layer with salt and pepper. Sprinkle the bread crumbs on top and drizzle evenly with the melted butter. Bake at 350 degrees for 20 to 25 minutes.

Macaroni and Cheese

4 cups cooled cooked macaroni
2 cups sour cream
1/2 cup (1 stick) butter, melted
1 1/2 cups heavy cream
4 cups shredded Cheddar cheese
Salt and pepper to taste
2 cups crumbled toasted bread

Combine the macaroni, sour cream, butter, cream and cheese in a large bowl. Season with salt and pepper. Stir to mix well. Pour into a buttered 9×13-inch baking dish. Top with the crumbled bread. Bake at 350 degrees for 20 to 25 minutes or until hot.

Note: This is really different! Our customers love this macaroni and cheese.

Corny Corn Bread

1 (8-ounce) can cream-style corn
1 cup buttermilk
2 eggs, lightly beaten
1/3 cup vegetable oil
1 (4-ounce) can chopped green chiles
1 1/2 cups (6 ounces) shredded Cheddar cheese
2 cups self-rising cornmeal
1/4 teaspoon baking soda

Mix the corn, buttermilk, eggs, oil, green chiles and cheese in a bowl. Mix the cornmeal and baking soda in a large bowl. Make a well in the center and pour in the buttermilk mixture. Stir just until moistened. Heat a cast-iron skillet or corn bread stick pans in a 450 degree oven until hot. Coat the hot pan with nonstick cooking spray or olive oil and spoon the batter into the pan. Bake at 350 degrees for 30 to 40 minutes for the skillet or 15 minutes for the corn bread stick pans, or until golden brown. Remove to a wire rack to cool.

Corn Fritters

2^1/$_2$ cups cornmeal mix
^{1}/$_4$ teaspoon black pepper
^{1}/$_4$ teaspoon cayenne pepper
^{1}/$_4$ cup finely chopped onion
2 tablespoons finely chopped green bell pepper
1 (2-ounce) jar diced pimento, drained
1 (8-ounce) can cream-style corn
^{1}/$_2$ cup boiling water
Vegetable oil for frying

Combine the cornmeal mix, black pepper, cayenne pepper, onion, bell pepper, pimento and corn in a large bowl. Stir to mix well. Stir in the boiling water. Let stand for 10 minutes. Heat ^{1}/$_4$ inch of oil in a large skillet. Drop tablespoons of batter into the hot oil, using a tablespoon that has been dipped in hot water. Fry over medium heat for 1 minute per side or until golden brown. Remove to paper towels to drain.

Cakes at Cherries are luscious —
a worthwhile indulgence.

Cakes at Cherries
tempt even the strongest soul.
Who can resist the Caramel
Cake—just like your grandmother
made—sliced still warm; or
the Fresh Strawberry Pound
Cake—when North Carolina
strawberries are in?

Pound cakes,
layer cakes, cheesecakes,
sheet cakes—it's all good.
Nothing stays around long
because we use real
ingredients. One thing
you'll never regret is a
piece of cake at Cherries.

Cakes

Old-Fashioned Chocolate Cake

Serves 12

4 ounces German's sweet chocolate
1/2 cup water
2 cups all-purpose flour
1 teaspoon baking soda
1/4 teaspoon salt
1 cup (2 sticks) butter or
  margarine, softened

2 cups sugar
4 egg yolks
1 teaspoon vanilla extract
1 cup buttermilk
4 egg whites
Chocolate Frosting (below)

Combine the chocolate and water in a microwave-safe bowl. Microwave until the chocolate is almost melted. Stir until the chocolate is melted and the mixture is smooth. Mix the flour, baking soda and salt together. Combine the butter and sugar in a large bowl. Beat with an electric mixer at medium speed until light and fluffy. Add the egg yolks, 1 at a time, beating well after each addition. Stir in the chocolate mixture and vanilla. Beat in the dry ingredients alternately with the buttermilk. Beat the egg whites in a bowl until stiff peaks form. Fold gently into the batter. Pour into 4 greased and floured cake pans. Bake at 350 degrees for 20 to 25 minutes or until the center springs back when lightly touched. Cool in the pans for 10 minutes. Remove to a wire rack to cool completely. Spread the Chocolate Frosting between the layers and over the top and side of the cake.

Chocolate Frosting

1 cup (2 sticks) butter
2 cups granulated sugar
1/2 cup baking cocoa

1 cup heavy cream
1 teaspoon vanilla extract
1 cup confectioners' sugar

Combine the butter, granulated sugar, baking cocoa, cream and vanilla in a saucepan. Cook over medium heat for 5 minutes or until thick, stirring often. Remove from the heat and beat in the confectioners' sugar.

Note: This is everybody's favorite!

132

Milk chocolate cake

4 ounces German's sweet chocolate
1/4 cup warm water
1 cup (2 sticks) butter or margarine, softened
8 ounces cream cheese, softened
1 (32-ounce) package confectioners' sugar
1 teaspoon vanilla extract
2 1/4 cups sifted all-purpose flour
1 teaspoon baking soda
1 teaspoon salt
1/4 cup (1/2 stick) butter or margarine, softened
3 eggs
1 cup buttermilk

Combine the chocolate and warm water in a saucepan. Cook over medium heat until the chocolate is melted and smooth, stirring often. Remove from the heat. Combine 1 cup butter, the cream cheese and confectioners' sugar in a large bowl. Beat with an electric mixer until light and fluffy. Add the melted chocolate and vanilla and beat until light and fluffy. Remove 3 cups and set aside to frost the cake. Mix the flour, baking soda and salt together. Add 1/4 cup butter to the remaining cream cheese mixture and beat until fluffy. Add the eggs, 1 at a time, beating well after each addition. Beat in the dry ingredients alternately with the buttermilk. Pour into 3 greased and floured 9-inch cake pans. Bake at 350 degrees for 25 minutes or until a wooden pick inserted in the center comes out clean. Cool in the pans for 10 minutes. Remove to a wire rack to cool completely. Spread the reserved chocolate mixture between the layers and over the top and side of the cake.

Note: This is a wonderful cake. It stays fresh and can be made ahead for parties.

Milky Way Cake

½ cup (1 stick) butter
8 (2-ounce) Milky Way candy bars
1¼ cups buttermilk
½ teaspoon baking soda
½ cup (1 stick) butter, softened
2 cups sugar

4 eggs
1 teaspoon vanilla extract
3 cups all-purpose flour
1 cup chopped pecans
Milk Chocolate Frosting (below)

Melt ½ cup butter in a saucepan. Add the candy bars. Cook over low heat until the candy bars melt, stirring constantly. Remove from the heat and let cool. Mix the buttermilk and baking soda in a small bowl. Beat ½ cup butter and the sugar in a large bowl until light and fluffy. Add the eggs, 1 at a time, beating well after each addition. Stir in the vanilla. Beat in the flour alternately with the buttermilk mixture, beating well after each addition. Stir in the melted candy bars and pecans. Pour into a greased and floured bundt pan. Bake at 325 degrees for 1 hour and 20 minutes or until a wooden pick inserted in the center comes out clean. Cool in the pan for 1 hour. Remove to a wire rack to cool completely. Frost with the Milk Chocolate Frosting.

Milk Chocolate Frosting

½ cup (1 stick) butter
2½ cups sugar
1 cup evaporated milk

1 cup chocolate chips
1 cup marshmallow creme

Melt the butter in a heavy saucepan. Stir in the sugar and evaporated milk. Cook over medium heat to 234 to 240 degrees on a candy thermometer, soft-ball stage, stirring often. Remove from the heat and add the chocolate chips and marshmallow creme. Beat until smooth, thinning with milk if necessary.

Note: This frosting works well on any cake!

Tunnel of Fudge Cake

1 3/4 cups (3 1/2 sticks) butter or
  margarine, softened
1 3/4 cups granulated sugar
6 eggs
2 cups confectioners' sugar
3/4 cup baking cocoa

1/2 teaspoon salt
2 1/4 cups all-purpose flour
2 cups toasted chopped walnuts
  (optional)
Chocolate Glaze (below)

Combine the butter and sugar in a large bowl. Beat with an electric mixer until light and fluffy. Add the eggs, 1 at a time, beating well after each addition. Beat in the confectioners' sugar, baking cocoa, salt and flour gradually at low speed. Stir in the walnuts. Pour into a greased and floured bundt pan. Bake at 350 degrees for 1 hour and 15 minutes or until a wooden pick inserted in the center comes out clean. Pour the Chocolate Glaze over the warm cake.

Chocolate Glaze

3/4 cup confectioners' sugar
1/4 cup baking cocoa
1 teaspoon to 2 tablespoons milk

Mix the confectioners' sugar and baking cocoa in a bowl. Stir in the milk to desired consistency.

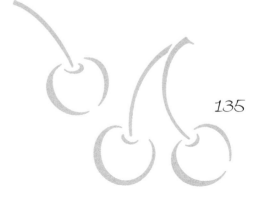

Devil's Food Cake

2 1/2 cups cake flour
1 cup baking cocoa
2 teaspoons baking soda
1/2 teaspoon salt
1 cup (2 sticks) butter or margarine,
  softened

2 cups sugar
1 teaspoon vanilla extract
3/4 teaspoon almond extract
2 eggs
2 1/4 cups buttermilk
Buttercream Frosting (below)

Mix the flour, baking cocoa, baking soda and salt together. Combine the butter, sugar, vanilla and almond extract in a large bowl. Beat with an electric mixer at medium speed until light and fluffy. Add the eggs, 1 at a time, beating well after each addition. Beat in the dry ingredients alternately with the buttermilk. Beat for 1 minute. Pour into 4 greased and floured 9-inch cake pans. Bake at 350 degrees for 20 to 25 minutes or until a wooden pick inserted in the center comes out clean. Cool in the pans for 10 minutes. Remove to a wire rack to cool completely. Spread the Buttercream Frosting between the layers and over the top and side of the cake. Garnish with sliced almonds.

Buttercream Frosting

1 cup (2 sticks) butter or margarine,
  softened
6 cups confectioners' sugar

1 1/2 teaspoons vanilla extract
3/4 teaspoon almond extract
4 to 6 tablespoons milk

Combine the butter, confectioners' sugar, vanilla, almond extract and milk in a large bowl. Beat with an electric mixer at medium speed until light and fluffy.

Note: This cake is also delicious with Coffee Buttercream on page 141.

Coca-Cola Cake

1/2 cup buttermilk
1 teaspoon baking soda
2 cups all-purpose flour
2 cups sugar
1/2 cup (1 stick) butter
1/2 cup vegetable oil

3 tablespoons baking cocoa
1 cup Coca-Cola
2 eggs, beaten
1 teaspoon vanilla extract
1/2 cup miniature marshmallows
Coca-Cola Icing (below)

Mix the buttermilk and baking soda in a small bowl. Let stand for at least 5 minutes. Sift the flour and sugar into a large bowl. Combine the butter, oil, baking cocoa and Coca-Cola in a saucepan. Bring to a boil, stirring occasionally. Pour into the dry ingredients and stir to mix well. Stir in the buttermilk mixture. Add the eggs, vanilla and marshmallows. Stir to mix well. Pour into a greased and floured 9×13-inch baking pan. Bake at 350 degrees for 45 minutes or until a wooden pick inserted in the center comes out clean. Remove to a wire rack to cool completely. Frost with the Coca-Cola Icing.

Coca-Cola Icing

1/2 cup (1 stick) butter
3 tablespoons baking cocoa
6 tablespoons Coca-Cola

1 (16-ounce) package confectioners'
  sugar
1 teaspoon vanilla extract
1 cup chopped nuts

Combine the butter, baking cocoa and Coca-Cola in a saucepan. Bring to a boil, stirring occasionally. Remove from the heat and add the confectioners' sugar, vanilla and nuts. Beat until creamy.

Decadent Fudge Cake

1 cup buttermilk
1/2 teaspoon baking soda
1 cup (2 sticks) butter, softened
1 1/2 cups sugar
4 eggs
2 1/2 cups all-purpose flour
1 cup semisweet chocolate chips
1/3 cup chocolate syrup

8 ounces German's sweet chocolate,
    melted and cooled
2 teaspoons vanilla extract
4 ounces white chocolate, chopped
2 tablespoons shortening
1/2 cup semisweet chocolate chips
2 teaspoons shortening

Mix the buttermilk and baking soda in a small bowl. Beat the butter and sugar in a large bowl until light and fluffy. Add the eggs, 1 at a time, beating well after each addition. Beat in the flour alternately with the buttermilk mixture, beginning and ending with the flour. Add 1 cup chocolate chips, the chocolate syrup, melted sweet chocolate and vanilla. Stir just until blended. Pour into a greased and floured bundt pan. Bake a 300 degrees for 1 hour and 25 minutes to 1 hour and 35 minutes or until a wooden pick inserted in the center comes out clean. Remove the cake from the pan immediately to a wire rack and let cool completely. Combine the white chocolate and 2 tablespoons shortening in a microwave-safe bowl. Microwave until melted and smooth, stirring often. Drizzle over the cooled cake. Combine 1/2 cup chocolate chips and 2 teaspoons shortening in a microwave-safe bowl. Microwave until melted and smooth, stirring often. Drizzle over the white chocolate.

chocolate velvet cake

2 cups all-purpose flour
1 teaspoon baking soda
1/2 teaspoon salt
1/2 cup (1 stick) butter, softened
1 (16-ounce) package light brown sugar
3 eggs
1 1/2 cups semisweet chocolate
  chips, melted

1 cup sour cream
1 cup hot water
2 teaspoons vanilla extract
2 cups white chocolate chips, melted
1 cup sliced almonds
Vanilla Frosting (below)

Sift the flour, baking soda and salt together. Combine the butter and brown sugar in a large bowl. Beat with an electric mixer until light and fluffy. Add the eggs, 1 at a time, beating well after each addition. Beat in the melted semisweet chocolate. Beat in the dry ingredients alternately with the sour cream, beginning and ending with the dry ingredients. Add the hot water in a slow steady stream, beating constantly at low speed. Beat just until blended. Stir in the vanilla. Pour into 3 greased and floured 9-inch cake pans. Bake at 350 degrees for 20 to 25 minutes or until a wooden pick inserted in the center comes out clean. Cool in the pans for 10 minutes. Remove to a wire rack to cool completely. Spread the melted white chocolate 1/4-inch thick on a foil-lined baking sheet. Press the almonds into the white chocolate. Chill for 30 minutes or until firm. Cut into chunks with a sharp knife. Spread the Vanilla Frosting between the layers and over the top and side of the cake. Press the almond chunks onto the frosting.

Vanilla Frosting

1 cup (2 sticks) butter, softened
1 (32-ounce) package
  confectioners' sugar

2/3 cup milk
1 tablespoon vanilla extract

Beat the butter in a bowl with an electric mixer until creamy. Beat in the confectioners' sugar alternately with the milk. Beat in the vanilla. Beat until fluffy.

Note: This is an all-around great chocolate cake and can be used with any frosting.

chocolate Upside-Down cake

3/4 cup all-purpose flour

2/3 cup sugar

3 tablespoons baking cocoa

1 1/2 teaspoons baking powder

1/2 teaspoon salt

1/2 cup milk

1 teaspoon vanilla extract

1/4 cup (1/2 stick) plus 1 teaspoon butter, softened

1/2 cup granulated sugar

1/2 cup packed light brown sugar

2 tablespoons baking cocoa

1/4 teaspoon salt

1 1/2 cups boiling water

Combine the flour, 2/3 cup sugar, 3 tablespoons baking cocoa, the baking powder, 1/2 teaspoon salt, the milk, vanilla and butter in a bowl. Beat with an electric mixer at medium speed to mix well. Pour into a nonstick 8×8-inch baking pan. Mix 1/2 cup granulated sugar, the brown sugar, 2 tablespoons baking cocoa and 1/4 teaspoon salt in a bowl. Sprinkle over the batter in the pan. Pour the boiling water evenly over the top; do not stir. Bake at 350 degrees for 1 hour. Remove to a wire rack. Serve warm with vanilla ice cream.

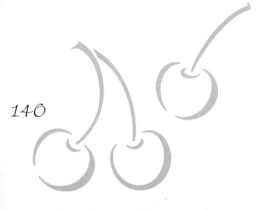

chocolate chiffon cake

6 ounces bittersweet chocolate, chopped
3/4 cup water
2 1/2 cups cake flour, sifted
2 teaspoons baking soda
1/8 teaspoon salt

1 cup (2 sticks) butter, softened
2 cups sugar
4 eggs
2 teaspoons vanilla extract
1 1/2 cups sour cream
Coffee Buttercream (below)

Combine the chocolate and water in a microwave-safe bowl. Microwave until the chocolate melts, stirring until smooth. Mix the flour, baking soda and salt together. Beat the butter and sugar in a large bowl until light and fluffy. Add the eggs, 1 at a time, beating well after each addition. Add the melted chocolate and vanilla. Stir just until combined. Stir in the dry ingredients alternately with the sour cream, beginning and ending with the dry ingredients. Pour into 4 greased and floured 9-inch cake pans. Bake at 350 degrees for 20 to 25 minutes or until a wooden pick inserted in the center comes out clean. Cool in the pans for 10 minutes. Remove to a wire rack to cool completely. Spread the Coffee Buttercream between 2 layers and over the top and side of the cake to make 2 cakes.

Coffee Buttercream

4 to 5 tablespoons instant coffee granules
3 tablespoons hot water

1 cup (2 sticks) butter, softened
6 cups confectioners' sugar

Dissolve the coffee granules in the hot water in a small bowl. Beat the butter in a bowl until creamy. Beat in the coffee and confectioners' sugar gradually. Beat until smooth.

Apple Dapple Cake

3 cups all-purpose flour
1 teaspoon baking soda
1 teaspoon salt
1 teaspoon ground cinnamon
1½ cups vegetable oil
2 cups sugar

3 eggs
2 teaspoons vanilla extract
3 cups finely chopped peeled apples
1 cup chopped nuts (optional)
1 cup flaked coconut (optional)
Vanilla Glaze (below)

Mix the flour, baking soda, salt and cinnamon together. Beat the oil, sugar and eggs in a large bowl until creamy. Beat in the dry ingredients. Stir in the apples, nuts and coconut. Pour into a greased and floured bundt pan. Bake at 350 degrees for 1 hour or until a wooden pick inserted in the center comes out clean. Cool in the pan for 10 minutes. Remove to a wire rack. Pour the Vanilla Glaze over the hot cake.

Vanilla Glaze

½ cup (1 stick) butter or margarine
1 cup packed brown sugar

¼ cup milk or rum
1 teaspoon vanilla extract

Mix the butter, brown sugar, milk and vanilla in a saucepan. Bring to a boil over medium heat. Boil for 2 minutes, stirring often.

Chocolate Banana Cake

Serves 12

3 cups cake flour
2 teaspoons baking powder
1/4 teaspoon baking soda
1/4 teaspoon salt
1 cup (2 sticks) butter, softened
2 1/4 cups sugar
3 eggs

2 ounces unsweetened chocolate, melted
1 cup buttermilk
1 cup mashed bananas
1 tablespoon vanilla extract
1 cup chopped pecans (optional)
Chocolate Frosting

Mix the flour, baking powder, baking soda and salt together. Combine the butter and sugar in a large bowl. Beat until light and fluffy. Add the eggs, 1 at a time, beating well after each addition. Beat in the chocolate. Beat in the dry ingredients alternately with the buttermilk. Stir in the bananas, vanilla and pecans. Pour into 3 greased and floured 9-inch cake pans. Bake at 350 degrees for 30 minutes or until a wooden pick inserted in the center comes out clean. Cool in the pans for 10 minutes. Remove to a wire rack to cool completely. Spread the Chocolate Frosting between the layers and over the top and side of the cake.

Chocolate Frosting

5 1/3 tablespoons butter, softened
5 cups sifted confectioners' sugar
1/3 cup baking cocoa

1/8 teaspoon salt
1/2 cup evaporated milk

Beat the butter, confectioners' sugar, baking cocoa and salt in a bowl. Beat in the milk gradually. Beat until smooth.

Note: This is a very moist cake.

Marvelous Banana Cake

3³/4 cups all-purpose flour
2 teaspoons baking soda
1 cup (2 sticks) butter or margarine, softened
3 cups sugar
2 cups mashed bananas
4 eggs, beaten
1 cup buttermilk
1 teaspoon vanilla extract
2 tablespoons bourbon or orange juice
1 cup pecans, chopped
Caramel Frosting (page 149)

Mix the flour and baking soda together. Combine the butter and sugar in a large bowl. Beat with an electric mixer at medium speed until light and fluffy. Beat in the bananas. Stir in the eggs. Stir in the dry ingredients alternately with the buttermilk, beginning and ending with the dry ingredients. Stir in the vanilla, bourbon and pecans. Pour into 4 greased and floured 9-inch cake pans. Bake at 350 degrees for 30 minutes or until a wooden pick inserted in the center comes out clean. Cool in the pans for 10 minutes. Remove to a wire rack to cool completely. Spread the Caramel Frosting between the layers and over the top and side of the cake.

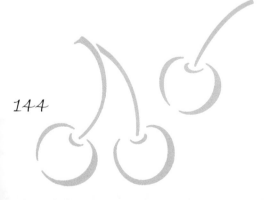

Butterscotch Cake

²/3 cup butterscotch chips
¹/4 cup water
2¹/4 cups all-purpose flour
1 teaspoon salt
1 teaspoon baking soda
¹/2 teaspoon baking powder

¹/2 cup (1 stick) butter, softened
1 cup sugar
3 eggs
1 cup buttermilk
Coconut Frosting (below)
1 cup heavy whipping cream, whipped

Combine the butterscotch chips and water in a small saucepan. Cook over low heat until the butterscotch melts, stirring constantly. Remove from the heat. Mix the flour, salt, baking soda and baking powder together. Combine the butter and sugar in a large bowl. Beat with an electric mixer until light and fluffy. Add the eggs, 1 at a time, beating well after each addition. Beat in the dry ingredients alternately with the buttermilk at low speed. Pour into 2 greased and floured 9-inch cake pans. Bake at 375 degrees for 20 to 25 minutes or until a wooden pick inserted in the center comes out clean. Cool in the pans for 10 minutes. Remove to a wire rack to cool completely. Spread the Coconut Frosting between the layers and over the top of the cake. Spread the whipped cream over the side of the cake.

Coconut Frosting

¹/2 cup sugar
1 tablespoon cornstarch
³/4 cup evaporated milk

5¹/3 tablespoons butter
1 cup flaked coconut
¹/2 cup chopped nuts

Mix the sugar and cornstarch in a saucepan. Stir in the evaporated milk. Cook over medium heat until thickened and boiling, stirring constantly. Remove from the heat and add the butter, coconut and nuts. Stir until the butter melts. Let cool.

carrot sheet cake

Serves 15

2 cups cake flour, sifted
2 teaspoons baking powder
2 teaspoons baking soda
2 teaspoons ground cinnamon
2 cups sugar
4 eggs

1 1/3 cups vegetable oil
4 cups grated carrots
3/4 cup chopped nuts
Cream Cheese Frosting (below)
Chopped pecans

Mix the flour, baking powder, baking soda and cinnamon together. Beat the sugar and eggs in a large bowl until thick and pale yellow. Stir in the oil. Add the dry ingredients and stir to mix well. Fold in the carrots and nuts. Spoon into a greased and floured 9×13-inch baking pan. Bake at 350 degrees for 30 to 40 minutes or until a wooden pick inserted in the center comes out clean. Remove to a wire rack to cool completely. Frost with the Cream Cheese Frosting and sprinkle with chopped pecans.

Note: This cake is delicious with Caramel Frosting (page 149) instead of the Cream Cheese Frosting. Many of our customers prefer the boiled Caramel Frosting.

Cream Cheese Frosting

8 ounces cream cheese, softened
1/2 cup (1 stick) butter, softened
1 teaspoon vanilla extract
1 (16-ounce) package confectioners' sugar

Beat the cream cheese and butter in a bowl until creamy. Add the vanilla and confectioners' sugar. Beat until smooth.

Pineapple Coconut Cake

1 (15-ounce) can crushed pineapple in
    juice, drained and juice reserved
1/2 cup lemon-lime soda
1 1/2 cups (3 sticks) butter or
    margarine, softened
3 cups sugar
5 eggs
3 cups cake flour, sifted

1 teaspoon vanilla extract
1 teaspoon lemon extract
2 cups sugar
1/4 cup cornstarch
1 cup water
Pineapple Cream Cheese Frosting (below)
1/2 cup flaked coconut

Mix 1/2 cup reserved pineapple juice and the lemon-lime soda in a small bowl. Beat the butter in a large bowl with an electric mixer at medium speed until creamy. Beat in 3 cups sugar gradually. Add the eggs, 1 at a time, beating well after each addition. Beat in the flour alternately with the lemon-lime soda mixture, beginning and ending with the flour. Stir in the vanilla and lemon extract. Pour into 3 greased and floured 9-inch cake pans. Bake at 350 degrees for 25 to 30 minutes or until a wooden pick inserted in the center comes out clean. Cool in the pans for 10 minutes. Remove to a wire rack to cool completely. Mix 2 cups sugar and the cornstarch in a saucepan. Stir in 1 cup drained pineapple and water. Cook over low heat for 15 minutes or until very thick, stirring occasionally. Remove from the heat and let cool. Spread between the layers and over the top of the cake. Spread the Pineapple Cream Cheese Frosting over the side of the cake. Sprinkle the flaked coconut over the frosting.

Pineapple Cream Cheese Frosting

1/2 cup (1 stick) butter, softened
3 ounces cream cheese, softened
1 (16-ounce) package confectioners'
    sugar, sifted

1 teaspoon vanilla extract
3 to 4 tablespoons reserved
    pineapple juice

Combine the butter and cream cheese in a bowl. Beat with an electric mixer at medium speed until smooth. Beat in the confectioners' sugar, vanilla and enough pineapple juice to make a good spreading consistency.

Note: This is a beautiful cake that holds well. It's great for company!

ollie's coconut cake

2 cups all-purpose flour
1 heaping teaspoon baking powder
1/8 teaspoon salt
1 cup (2 sticks) butter or margarine,
    softened
1 1/2 cups sugar
1 egg
4 egg yolks

1 cup milk
1 teaspoon vanilla extract
Milk of 1 fresh coconut, strained
Grated meat of 1 fresh coconut
1 1/2 cups sugar
4 egg whites
12 heaping tablespoons sugar

Mix the flour, baking powder and salt together. Beat the butter and 1 1/2 cups sugar in a large bowl until light and fluffy. Add the egg and egg yolks, 1 at a time, beating well after each addition. Beat in the dry ingredients alternately with the milk, beginning and ending with the dry ingredients. Stir in the vanilla. Pour into 4 greased and floured cake pans. Bake at 350 degrees for 15 to 20 minutes or until a wooden pick inserted in the center comes out clean. Cool in the pans for 10 minutes. Remove to a wire rack. Mix the coconut milk, grated coconut and 1 1/2 cups sugar in a saucepan. Bring to a boil, stirring often. Remove from the heat and spread between the layers of the cake. Combine the egg whites and 12 tablespoons sugar in the top of a double boiler. Cook over boiling water, beating with an electric mixer until thick and shiny. Remove from the heat and spread over the top and side of the cake.

Note: This is a delicate cake that is definitely worth the effort. We love it hot from the oven. This is the cake used for the caramel and the lemon cake. It also makes a great shortcake—awesome!

ollie's caramel cake

2 cups all-purpose flour
1 heaping teaspoon baking powder
1/8 teaspoon salt
1 cup (2 sticks) butter or margarine,
  softened
1 1/2 cups sugar

1 egg
4 egg yolks
1 cup milk
1 teaspoon vanilla extract
Caramel Frosting (below)

Mix the flour, baking powder and salt together. Beat the butter and 1 1/2 cups sugar in a large bowl until light and fluffy. Add the egg and egg yolks, 1 at a time, beating well after each addition. Beat in the dry ingredients alternately with the milk, beginning and ending with the dry ingredients. Stir in the vanilla. Pour into 4 greased and floured cake pans. Bake at 350 degrees for 15 to 20 minutes or until a wooden pick inserted in the center comes out clean. Cool in the pans for 10 minutes. Remove to a wire rack. Spread the warm Caramel Frosting between the layers, allowing each layer to cool before proceeding. (The Caramel Frosting must cool before adding another layer or the layers will slide. Reheat the Caramel Frosting if it becomes hard to spread.) Spread the remaining Caramel Frosting over the top and side of the cake.

Caramel Frosting

1 cup (2 sticks) butter
1 cup heavy cream
1 (16-ounce) package brown sugar

1 (16-ounce) package
  confectioners' sugar

Bring the butter, cream and brown sugar to a boil in a heavy saucepan. Boil for 5 minutes or until thickened and the sugar is dissolved, stirring often. Pour carefully into a large bowl and add the confectioners' sugar immediately. Beat until creamy.

Note: This is a great old-fashioned cake but a bit difficult to make.

Ollie's Lemon Layer Cake

2 cups all-purpose flour
1 heaping teaspoon baking powder
1/8 teaspoon salt
1 cup (2 sticks) butter or margarine,
   softened
1 1/2 cups sugar
1 egg
4 egg yolks

1 cup milk
1 teaspoon vanilla extract
2 (14-ounce) cans sweetened
   condensed milk
1 cup freshly squeezed lemon juice
3 cups heavy whipping cream
4 teaspoons grated lemon zest

Mix the flour, baking powder and salt together. Beat the butter and 1 1/2 cups sugar in a large bowl until light and fluffy. Add the egg and egg yolks, 1 at a time, beating well after each addition. Beat in the dry ingredients alternately with the milk, beginning and ending with the dry ingredients. Stir in the vanilla. Pour into 4 greased and floured cake pans. Bake at 350 degrees for 15 to 20 minutes or until a wooden pick inserted in the center comes out clean. Cool in the pans for 10 minutes. Remove to a wire rack. Mix the sweetened condensed milk and lemon juice in a bowl. Beat the cream in a large bowl until stiff peaks form. Fold in the lemon juice mixture. Spread between the layers and over the top and side of the cake. Sprinkle with the lemon zest. Chill until cold. Let stand at room temperature for 30 minutes before serving.

Note: This is so light and lemony!

Pumpkin Gingerbread with Caramel Sauce

Serves 9

2 1/4 cups all-purpose flour
1/2 cup sugar
10 2/3 tablespoons butter or margarine
3/4 cup chopped pecans
3/4 cup buttermilk
1/2 cup canned pumpkin
1/2 cup molasses

1 egg
1 teaspoon baking soda
1/4 teaspoon salt
1 1/2 teaspoons ginger
1/2 teaspoon ground cinnamon
1/4 teaspoon ground cloves
Caramel Sauce (below)

Mix the flour and sugar in a bowl. Cut in the butter with a pastry blender or fork until crumbly. Stir in the pecans. Remove 1 1/4 cups and press onto the bottom of an ungreased 9×9-inch baking pan. Add the buttermilk, pumpkin, molasses, egg, baking soda, salt, ginger, cinnamon and cloves to the remaining crumb mixture in the bowl. Beat with an electric mixer at low speed until blended. Pour over the crumb mixture in the pan. Bake at 350 degrees for 40 minutes or until the center is set. Remove to a wire rack to cool completely. Cut into squares and serve with the Carmel Sauce and ice cream.

Caramel Sauce

1/2 cup (1 stick) butter or margarine
1 1/4 cups packed brown sugar

2 tablespoons light corn syrup
1/2 cup heavy cream

Melt the butter in a small heavy saucepan over low heat. Stir in the brown sugar and corn syrup. Bring to a boil, stirring constantly. Boil for 1 minute or until the sugar dissolves, stirring constantly. Stir in the cream gradually. Return to a boil. Remove from the heat and let cool.

Hurricane Cake

1½ cups sifted all-purpose flour
1 scant teaspoon baking soda
1 teaspoon ground cinnamon
1¼ cups boiling water
1 cup rolled oats
½ cup vegetable oil
1 cup granulated sugar
1 cup packed brown sugar
2 eggs
1 teaspoon vanilla extract
6 tablespoons margarine, melted
1 cup packed brown sugar
¼ cup evaporated milk
1 cup flaked coconut
½ cup chopped nuts

Mix the flour, baking soda and cinnamon together. Pour the boiling water over the oats in a bowl. Let stand for 20 minutes. Beat the oil, granulated sugar and 1 cup brown sugar in a large bowl. Beat in the eggs. Stir in the oatmeal mixture. Stir in the dry ingredients. Stir in the vanilla. Pour into a greased and floured 9×13-inch baking pan. Bake at 350 degrees for 30 to 40 minutes or until a wooden pick inserted in the center comes out clean. Remove to a wire rack to cool. Combine the margarine, 1 cup brown sugar, the evaporated milk, coconut and nuts in a bowl. Stir to mix well. Spread over the cake. Place under a broiler until bubbly. Remove to a wire rack to cool.

Note: This is one of Linda's favorites.

Brown Sugar Pound Cake

3 cups all-purpose flour
1/2 teaspoon baking powder
1/2 teaspoon salt
1 cup (2 sticks) margarine, softened
1/2 cup shortening
1 cup granulated sugar
1 (16-ounce) package light brown sugar
5 eggs
1 cup milk
1 teaspoon vanilla extract
1 cup chopped nuts, coated in flour

Sift the flour, baking powder and salt together. Combine the margarine, shortening, granulated sugar and brown sugar in a large bowl. Beat until light and fluffy. Add the eggs, 1 at a time, beating well after each addition. Beat in the dry ingredients alternately with the milk. Stir in the vanilla and nuts. Pour into a greased and lightly floured 10-inch tube pan. Bake at 350 degrees for 10 minutes. Reduce the heat to 325 degrees. Bake for 45 to 50 minutes or until a wooden pick inserted in the center comes out clean. Cool in the pan for 10 to 15 minutes. Remove to a wire rack to cool completely.

chocolate pound cake

3 cups all-purpose flour
1/2 cup baking cocoa
1/2 teaspoon baking powder
1/4 teaspoon salt
1 cup (2 sticks) butter, softened

1/2 cup shortening
3 cups sugar
5 eggs
1 1/4 cups milk
1 teaspoon vanilla extract

Sift the flour, baking cocoa, baking powder and salt together. Combine the butter, shortening and sugar in a large bowl. Beat until light and fluffy. Add the eggs, 1 at a time, beating well after each addition. Beat in the dry ingredients alternately with the milk and vanilla. Pour into a greased and lightly floured 10-inch tube pan. Bake at 325 degrees for 1 hour and 45 minutes to 2 hours or until a wooden pick inserted in the center comes out clean. Cool in the pan for 10 to 15 minutes. Remove to a wire rack to cool completely.

crusty cream cheese pound cake

1 cup (2 sticks) butter or
    margarine, softened
1/2 cup shortening
3 cups sugar

8 ounces cream cheese, softened
3 cups sifted cake flour
6 eggs
1 tablespoon vanilla extract

Combine the butter and shortening in a large bowl. Beat with an electric mixer at medium speed until creamy. Beat in the sugar gradually. Add the cream cheese and beat until light and fluffy. Beat in the flour alternately with the eggs, beginning and ending with the flour. Stir in the vanilla. Pour into a greased and lightly floured 10-inch tube pan. Bake at 325 degrees for 1 hour and 15 minutes or until a wooden pick inserted in the center comes out clean. Cool in the pan for 10 to 15 minutes. Remove to a wire rack to cool completely.

Note: This is our best pound cake. It's great with strawberries!

Orange Pound Cake

3 cups cake flour, sifted
1 tablespoon baking powder
1/4 teaspoon salt
1/2 cup fresh orange juice
1/2 cup water
1/2 cup (1 stick) butter, softened

2 cups sugar
7 egg yolks
1 teaspoon vanilla extract
7 egg whites
Orange Glaze (below)

Mix the flour, baking powder and salt together. Mix the orange juice and water in a small bowl. Beat the butter and sugar in a large bowl until light and fluffy. Add the egg yolks, 1 at a time, beating well after each addition. Beat in the dry ingredients alternately with the orange juice mixture, beginning and ending with the dry ingredients. Beat in the vanilla. Beat the egg whites in a bowl with an electric mixer at high speed until stiff peaks form. Fold into the batter. Pour into a greased and lightly floured 10-inch tube pan. Bake at 350 degrees for 40 minutes or until a wooden pick inserted in the center comes out clean. Cool in the pan for 10 to 15 minutes. Remove to a wire rack to cool completely. Spoon the Orange Glaze over the cake.

Orange Glaze

1 tablespoon grated orange zest
Juice of 2 large oranges
1 cup confectioners' sugar

Combine the orange zest, orange juice and confectioners' sugar in a bowl. Stir to mix well.

Fresh Peach Pound Cake

Serves 16

1 1/2 cups vegetable oil
2 cups sugar
3 eggs, beaten
2 teaspoons vanilla extract
3 cups self-rising flour

3 cups diced peeled fresh peaches
1 cup flaked coconut (optional)
1 cup chopped nuts, (optional)
Peach Cream Cheese Frosting (below)

Mix the oil and sugar in a large bowl. Stir in the eggs and vanilla. Stir in the flour. Stir in the peaches. Stir in the coconut and nuts. Pour into a greased and lightly floured bundt pan. Bake at 350 degrees for 1 hour or until a wooden pick inserted in the center comes out clean. Cool in the pan for 10 to 15 minutes. Remove to a wire rack to cool completely. Spoon the Peach Cream Cheese Frosting over the top of the cake and drizzle down the side.

Peach Cream Cheese Frosting

4 ounces cream cheese, softened
2 peaches, peeled, pitted and sliced
1/2 cup confectioners' sugar

Process the cream cheese, peaches and confectioners' sugar in a food processor until smooth.

Note: When peaches are ripe, we can't make enough of these cakes.

156

Fresh Strawberry Pound Cake

3 cups all-purpose flour
1/2 teaspoon baking powder
1 cup (2 sticks) butter, softened
1/2 cup shortening
2 1/2 cups sugar

6 eggs
1/2 cup milk
1 pound fresh strawberries, chopped
Strawberry Glaze (below)

Mix the flour and baking powder together. Combine the butter, shortening and sugar in a large bowl. Beat until light and fluffy. Add the eggs, 1 at a time, beating well after each addition. Beat in the dry ingredients alternately with the milk. Stir in the strawberries. Pour into a greased and lightly floured 10-inch tube pan. Bake at 350 degrees for 1 hour to 1 hour and 15 minutes or until a wooden pick inserted in the center comes out clean. Remove the cake from the pan immediately to a wire rack and let cool completely. Spoon the Strawberry Glaze over the cooled cake.

Strawberry Glaze

1 cup confectioners' sugar
1/4 cup milk
1/4 cup chopped fresh strawberries

Combine the confectioners' sugar, milk and strawberries in a bowl. Stir to mix well.

*Pies at cherries are really Southern —
a special treat.*

*P*ies at Cherries
melt in your mouth. Our pies
are traditional Southern fare
at its best. What tastes better
than a flaky piecrust filled
with rich chocolate custard
and topped with a glistening
meringue? Cherries collected
and tweaked these recipes
over thirty years. Each has its
own history.

Sweet potato,
brown sugar, lemon chess—
nothing tops off the end of a
meal like a piece of pie and
coffee at Cherries.

Pies

chocolate chess pie

2 cups sugar
2 tablespoons cornmeal
1/4 cup baking cocoa
5 eggs, lightly beaten
2/3 cup milk
1/2 cup (1 stick) butter, melted and cooled
1 teaspoon vanilla extract
1 unbaked (9-inch) pie shell
1/2 cup chopped walnuts (optional)

Mix the sugar, cornmeal and baking cocoa in a bowl. Add the eggs, milk, butter and vanilla. Stir to mix well. Pour into the pie shell. Sprinkle with the walnuts. Bake at 350 degrees for 45 minutes or until set. Remove to a wire rack to cool.

Buttermilk Coconut Chess Pie

3 eggs, lightly beaten
1 1/2 cups sugar
1/2 cup flaked coconut
1/2 cup buttermilk
2 tablespoons all-purpose flour
1 teaspoon vanilla extract
1/2 cup (1 stick) butter or margarine, melted
1 unbaked (9-inch) deep-dish pie shell

Combine the eggs, sugar, coconut, buttermilk, flour and vanilla in a bowl. Stir to mix well. Stir in the butter. Pour into the pie shell. Bake at 350 degrees until set. Remove to a wire rack to cool.

Lemon Chess Pie

2 cups sugar
1 tablespoon all-purpose flour
1 tablespoon cornmeal
¹/₄ teaspoon salt
¹/₄ cup (¹/₂ stick) butter or margarine, melted
2 teaspoons grated lemon zest
¹/₄ cup lemon juice
¹/₄ cup milk
4 eggs
1 unbaked (9-inch) pie shell

Mix the sugar, flour, cornmeal and salt in a bowl. Add the butter, lemon zest, lemon juice and milk. Stir to mix well. Add the eggs, 1 at a time, beating well after each addition. Pour into the pie shell. Bake at 350 degrees for 50 minutes. Remove to a wire rack to cool.

Note: This is a Southern delight!

Pineapple Coconut Chess Pie

Serves 6

1 1/2 cups sugar
3 tablespoons cornmeal
2 tablespoons all-purpose flour
1/4 teaspoon salt
4 eggs, lightly beaten
1 teaspoon vanilla extract
1/4 cup (1/2 stick) butter or margarine, melted
1 (15-ounce) can crushed pineapple, well drained
1 (3-ounce) can flaked coconut
1 unbaked (9-inch) pie shell

Mix the sugar, cornmeal, flour and salt in a bowl. Add the eggs and vanilla and stir to mix well. Stir in the butter, pineapple and coconut. Pour into the pie shell. Bake at 350 degrees for 1 hour or until set. Remove to a wire rack to cool.

Oatmeal Chess Pie

½ cup (1 stick) margarine, melted
1 cup light corn syrup
1 cup sugar
1 teaspoon vanilla extract
3 eggs, beaten
1 cup rolled oats
1 unbaked (9-inch) pie shell

Mix the margarine, corn syrup, sugar and vanilla in a bowl. Add the eggs and oats and stir to mix well. Pour into the pie shell. Bake at 350 degrees for 50 to 60 minutes or until set. Remove to a wire rack to cool.

Note: Try adding ½ cup chocolate chips for a different twist.

chocolate chip cookie pie

2 eggs
¹/2 cup all-purpose flour
¹/2 cup sugar
¹/2 cup packed light brown sugar
³/4 cup (1¹/2 sticks) butter, softened
1 cup chocolate chips
1 cup chopped nuts
1 unbaked (9-inch) pie shell

Beat the eggs in a bowl with an electric mixer at high speed until foamy. Beat in the flour, sugar and brown sugar. Beat in the butter. Stir in the chocolate chips and nuts. Pour into the pie shell. Bake at 325 degrees for 55 to 60 minutes or until a knife inserted in the center comes out clean. Remove to a wire rack to cool.

Schoolhouse Fudge Pie

1/2 cup (1 stick) margarine
1 cup semisweet chocolate chips
1/2 cup peanut butter
1 cup sugar
2 tablespoons all-purpose flour
2 eggs, beaten
1/4 cup milk
1/2 cup rolled oats
1 teaspoon vanilla extract
1 unbaked (9-inch) pie shell

Combine the margarine, chocolate chips and peanut butter in a saucepan. Cook over low heat until melted, stirring frequently. Remove from the heat and let cool slightly. Stir in the sugar, flour, eggs, milk, oats and vanilla. Pour into the pie shell. Bake at 350 degrees for 50 to 60 minutes or until set. Remove to a wire rack to cool.

Sweetheart Fudge Pie

¹/₂ cup (1 stick) butter or margarine, softened
³/₄ cup packed brown sugar
3 eggs
2 cups semisweet chocolate chips, melted
2 teaspoons instant coffee granules
1 teaspoon rum extract
¹/₂ cup all-purpose flour
1 cup walnuts, coarsely chopped
1 unbaked (9-inch) pie shell

Beat the butter in a bowl with an electric mixer at medium speed until creamy. Beat in the brown sugar gradually. Add the eggs, 1 at a time, beating well after each addition. Beat in the chocolate, coffee granules and rum extract. Stir in the flour and walnuts. Pour into the pie shell. Bake at 375 degrees for 25 minutes. Remove to a wire rack to cool completely. Cover and chill for 8 hours. Garnish with whipped cream and chopped walnuts.

Toll House Pie

1/2 cup (1 stick) butter, melted
1 cup sugar
1 cup light corn syrup
4 eggs, beaten
1 teaspoon vanilla extract
1/2 cup chopped pecans
1/2 cup semisweet chocolate chips
1 unbaked (9-inch) pie shell

Mix the butter, sugar and corn syrup together in a bowl. Stir in the eggs and vanilla. Stir in the pecans and chocolate chips. Pour into the pie shell. Bake at 350 degrees for 50 to 60 minutes or until set. Remove to a wire rack to cool.

Chocolate Cream Pie

Serves 6

1 cup sugar
¹/₄ cup plus 2 teaspoons cornstarch
¹/₈ teaspoon salt
3 cups milk
3 egg yolks, beaten
3 ounces bittersweet chocolate, melted
1¹/₂ tablespoons butter
Dash of vanilla extract
1 baked (9-inch) pie shell
Never-Fail Meringue (page 185)

Mix the sugar, cornstarch and salt in the top of a double boiler. Whisk in the milk and egg yolks. Cook over boiling water until beginning to thicken, stirring constantly. Stir in the chocolate. Cook until very thick, stirring constantly. Remove from the heat and add the butter and vanilla. Stir until the butter melts. Press a sheet of waxed paper onto the surface of the chocolate filling and let cool. Remove the waxed paper and pour the filling into the pie shell. Spread the Never Fail Meringue over the chocolate filling, sealing to the edge. Bake at 350 degrees for 10 to 12 minutes or until light brown and the egg white is cooked through. Remove to a wire rack to cool completely.

Brownie Fudge Pie

1/2 cup (1 stick) margarine
1 ounce unsweetened chocolate
1 cup sugar
2 eggs
2/3 cup cake flour
1 teaspoon vanilla extract
1/4 cup chopped pecans

      Combine the margarine and chocolate in a microwave-safe bowl. Microwave until melted, stirring until smooth. Let cool slightly. Stir in the sugar, eggs, flour and vanilla. Pour into a greased 9-inch pie plate. Sprinkle with the pecans. Bake at 350 degrees for 20 minutes or until the center is just set. Remove to a wire rack. Serve warm with vanilla ice cream.

Note: This recipe was a gift from Judy Yarborough at a recipe shower for Karol. It is one of our customer's favorites.

Coconut Caramel Pie

¼ cup (½ stick) butter
½ cup (or more) chopped pecans
1 (7-ounce) package (or more) flaked coconut
16 ounces cream cheese, softened
1 (14-ounce) can sweetened condensed milk
1 (16-ounce) container frozen whipped topping, thawed
2 baked (9-inch) pie shells, or 2 (9-inch) graham cracker
   pie shells
1 jar caramel ice cream topping

Melt the butter in a large skillet. Add the pecans and coconut and sauté until golden brown. Remove from the heat and let cool. Beat the cream cheese and sweetened condensed milk in a large bowl until smooth. Fold in the whipped topping. Spread half the cream cheese mixture in the pie shells. Sprinkle with half the coconut mixture and drizzle with half the caramel topping. Repeat the layers. Freeze until firm. Serve frozen.

Note: This pie is very rich and delicious. A little goes a long way. It's great to do ahead for company.

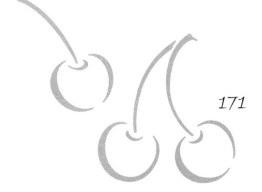

Coconut Cream Pie

3/4 cup sugar
1/4 cup plus 2 teaspoons cornstarch
1/8 teaspoon salt
3 egg yolks, beaten
3 cups milk
1 1/2 tablespoons butter
Dash of vanilla extract
3/4 cup flaked coconut
1 baked (9-inch) pie shell
Never-Fail Meringue (page 185)

Mix the sugar, cornstarch and salt in the top of a double
boiler. Whisk in the egg yolks and milk. Cook over boiling water until very thick, stirring
constantly. Remove from the heat and add the butter, vanilla and coconut. Stir until
the butter melts. Press a sheet of waxed paper onto the surface of the coconut filling
and chill. Remove the waxed paper and pour the filling into the pie shell. Spread the
Never-Fail Meringue over the coconut filling, sealing to the edge. Bake at 350 degrees
for 10 to 12 minutes or until the top is light brown and the egg white is cooked through.
Remove to a wire rack to cool completely.

Coconut Custard Pie

1 1/4 cups sugar
2 heaping tablespoons all-purpose flour
1/4 cup (1/2 stick) butter, melted
1 cup milk
2 eggs, beaten
6 ounces flaked coconut
1 unbaked (9-inch) pie shell

Mix the sugar and flour in a bowl. Stir in the butter, milk and eggs. Stir in the coconut. Pour into the pie shell. Bake at 350 degrees for 1 hour or until set. Remove to a wire rack to cool.

Note: This is the best coconut custard pie! The recipe was shared by a friend, Mr. Tise, over thirty years ago.

Golden Oatmeal Coconut Pie

1/4 cup (1/2 stick) margarine, softened
1/2 cup granulated sugar
1/2 cup packed light brown sugar
2 eggs
1 cup milk
3/4 cup light corn syrup
1 teaspoon vanilla extract
3/4 cup rolled oats
3/4 cup flaked coconut
1 unbaked (9-inch) pie shell

Combine the margarine, granulated sugar and brown sugar in a bowl. Beat until light and fluffy. Add the eggs, 1 at a time, beating well after each addition. Beat in the milk, corn syrup and vanilla. Stir in the oats and coconut. Pour into the pie shell. Bake at 350 degrees for 50 minutes or until set. Remove to a wire rack to cool.

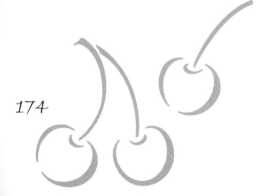

Exquisite Coconut Pie

2 eggs
1 cup sugar
$^1/_4$ cup ($^1/_2$ stick) butter, melted
$^1/_2$ cup milk
$^1/_2$ cup flaked coconut
$^1/_2$ cup pecans
1 teaspoon vanilla extract
1 unbaked (9-inch) pie shell

Beat the eggs in a bowl until foamy. Beat in the sugar and butter. Stir in the milk, coconut, pecans and vanilla. Pour into the pie shell. Bake at 350 degrees for 50 to 60 minutes or until set. Remove to a wire rack to cool.

Apple Crumb Pie

4 large tart apples, peeled, cored and
   cut into eighths
1 unbaked (9-inch) pie shell
1/2 cup sugar
1 teaspoon ground cinnamon
3/4 cup all-purpose flour
1/2 cup sugar
5 1/3 tablespoons butter

Arrange the apples in the pie shell. Mix 1/2 cup sugar and the cinnamon in a bowl. Sprinkle over the apples. Sift the flour and 1/2 cup sugar into a bowl. Cut in the butter with a pastry blender or fork until the mixture resembles cornmeal. Sprinkle over the apples. Bake at 450 degrees for 10 minutes. Reduce the heat to 350 degrees. Bake for 30 minutes or until the apples are tender. Remove to a wire rack to cool.

Apple Praline Pie

1 (2-crust) deep-dish pie pastry
4 to 6 cups thinly sliced peeled apples
3/4 cup granulated sugar
1/4 cup all-purpose flour
1 teaspoon ground cinnamon
1/4 teaspoon salt
2 tablespoons butter, cut into pieces
1/4 cup (1/2 stick) margarine, melted
1/2 cup packed brown sugar
2 tablespoons half-and-half
1/2 cup chopped pecans

Fit 1 pie pastry into a 9-inch deep-dish pie plate. Arrange the apples in the pie shell. Mix the granulated sugar, flour, cinnamon and salt in a bowl. Sprinkle over the apples. Dot with the butter. Top with the other pie pastry and flute the edges to seal. Cut slits in the top crust. Bake at 350 degrees for 50 to 55 minutes or until golden brown. Mix the margarine, brown sugar, half-and-half and pecans in a bowl. Spread over the top of the hot pie. Bake for 5 minutes longer. Remove to a wire rack and let cool for 1 hour before serving.

Cranberry Pecan Pie

3 eggs
1 cup dark corn syrup
2/3 cup sugar
6 tablespoons butter, melted
1 teaspoon vanilla extract
Pinch of salt
1 cup fresh cranberries, coarsely chopped
1 unbaked (9-inch) pie shell
1 cup pecan halves, toasted

Whisk the eggs, corn syrup and sugar in a bowl. Whisk in the butter, vanilla and salt. Stir in the cranberries. Pour into the pie shell. Arrange the pecans on top. Bake at 350 degrees for 50 to 60 minutes or until set. Remove to a wire rack to cool.

Note: This pie is great for fall and holidays.

Lemon Blueberry Fluff Pie

Serves 6

1 (14-ounce) can sweetened condensed milk
¹⁄₄ cup lemon juice
2 egg yolks, well beaten
2 egg whites
1 cup fresh blueberries
1 baked (9-inch) pie shell

Beat the sweetened condensed milk in a bowl. Add the lemon juice and beat to mix well. Add the egg yolks and beat to mix well. Beat the egg whites in a small bowl until stiff peaks form. Fold into the lemon mixture. Fold in the blueberries. Pour into the pie shell. Bake at 350 degrees for 20 minutes or until set. Remove to a wire rack to cool.

Peach Crumb Pie

1 cup granulated sugar
1/3 cup all-purpose flour
2 eggs, lightly beaten
1 1/3 cups sour cream
1 teaspoon vanilla extract
3 cups diced fresh or frozen peaches
1 unbaked (9-inch) pie shell
1/3 cup all-purpose flour
1/3 cup packed light brown sugar
5 1/3 tablespoons butter, softened
1/3 cup chopped pecans

Combine the sugar, 1/3 cup flour, the eggs, sour cream and vanilla in a large bowl. Stir until smooth. Fold in the peaches gradually. Spoon into the pie shell. Bake at 400 degrees for 45 to 50 minutes or until set. Mix 1/3 cup flour and brown sugar in a bowl. Cut in the butter with a pastry blender or fork until crumbly. Stir in the pecans. Sprinkle over the hot pie. Bake for 10 minutes longer or until golden brown. Remove to a wire rack to cool.

Note: We use this same recipe with raspberries or apples.

Sweet Potato Pie

2 cups mashed cooked sweet potatoes
2 tablespoons butter, softened
2 eggs
1 cup sugar
1 tablespoon all-purpose flour
$1/8$ teaspoon salt
$1/2$ cup buttermilk
$1/4$ teaspoon baking soda
1 teaspoon vanilla extract
1 unbaked (9-inch) pie shell

Combine the sweet potatoes, butter and eggs in a bowl. Stir to mix well. Mix the sugar, flour and salt in a bowl. Stir into the potato mixture. Mix the buttermilk and soda in a small bowl. Add to the potato mixture and stir to mix well. Stir in the vanilla. Pour into the pie shell. Bake at 350 degrees for 1 hour and 10 minutes or until set. Remove to a wire rack to cool.

Note: We bake our sweet potatoes for this pie.

Butterscotch Meringue Pie

1 1/2 cups packed brown sugar
3 tablespoons all-purpose flour
3 tablespoons cornstarch
2 cups cold milk
3 egg yolks
6 tablespoons butter
Dash of vanilla extract
1 baked (9-inch) deep-dish pie shell
Never-Fail Meringue (page 185)

Mix the brown sugar, flour and cornstarch together in the top of a double boiler. Whisk in the milk and egg yolks. Cook over boiling water until very thick, stirring constantly. Remove from the heat and add the butter and vanilla. Stir until the butter melts. Press a sheet of waxed paper onto the surface of the butterscotch filling and let cool. Remove the waxed paper and pour the filling into the pie shell. Spread the Never-Fail Meringue over the butterscotch filling, sealing to the edge. Bake at 350 degrees for 10 to 12 minutes or until the top is light brown and the egg white is cooked through. Remove to a wire rack to cool completely.

Note: This is a Southern classic. It is well worth the effort.

Brown Sugar Lemon Meringue Pie

1 tablespoon all-purpose flour
1 1/2 cups granulated sugar
2 teaspoons grated lemon zest
1 tablespoon cornmeal
4 eggs, beaten
1/3 cup milk
1/4 cup (1/2 stick) butter, melted
1/4 cup lemon juice
1 unbaked (9-inch) pie shell
2 egg whites, at room temperature
1 tablespoon lemon juice
1/2 cup packed light brown sugar

      Mix the flour, granulated sugar, lemon zest and cornmeal in a bowl. Add the eggs, milk, butter and 1/4 cup lemon juice. Beat to mix well. Pour into the pie shell. Bake at 350 degrees for 40 minutes or until set. Beat the egg whites in a bowl until doubled in volume. Beat in 1 tablespoon lemon juice. Beat in the brown sugar, 1 to 2 tablespoons at a time. Beat until stiff peaks form. Spread over the lemon filling, sealing to the edge. Bake at 400 degrees for 8 minutes or until golden brown and the egg white is cooked through. Remove to a wire rack to cool completely.

Strawberry Meringue Pie

3 egg whites
1 teaspoon vanilla extract
1/2 teaspoon baking powder
3/4 cup granulated sugar
3/4 cup coarsely chopped
   semisweet chocolate

1/2 cup chopped pecans
1 cup crushed butter crackers
1 cup heavy whipping cream
2 tablespoons sifted confectioners' sugar
1 teaspoon vanilla extract
2 cups sliced strawberries

Mix the egg whites, 1 teaspoon vanilla and the baking powder in a large bowl. Let stand for 30 minutes. Beat with an electric mixer at medium speed until soft peaks form. Beat in the granulated sugar, 1 tablespoon at a time. Beat until very stiff peaks form. Reserve 2 tablespoons of the chopped chocolate and place in a small bowl. Reserve 2 tablespoons of the chopped pecans and stir into the reserved chocolate. Chop the remaining pecans finely and place in a bowl. Add the remaining chopped chocolate and the crushed crackers. Stir to mix well. Fold into the egg white mixture. Spoon into a greased 9-inch pie plate, using a spoon to shape the mixture into a pie shell. Bake at 350 degrees for 25 minutes or until golden brown. Remove to a wire rack to cool completely. Combine the cream, confectioners' sugar and 1 teaspoon vanilla in a bowl. Beat with an electric mixer at low speed until soft peaks form. Fold in 1 1/2 cups of the strawberries. Spoon into the cooled meringue shell. Top with the remaining strawberries and sprinkle with the reserved chocolate mixture. Serve immediately or chill for up to 24 hours.

Never-Fail Meringue

1 tablespoon cornstarch
2 tablespoons cold water
1/2 cup boiling water
3 egg whites
6 tablespoons sugar
Pinch of salt
1 teaspoon vanilla extract

Mix the cornstarch and cold water together in a saucepan. Stir in the boiling water. Cook until thickened and clear, stirring constantly. Remove from the heat and let cool completely. Beat the egg whites in a bowl with an electric mixer at high speed until foamy. Beat in the sugar gradually. Beat until stiff, but not dry. Beat in the salt and vanilla at low speed. Beat in the cornstarch mixture gradually. Increase the speed to high and beat well.

Brown Sugar Pie

1 cup (2 sticks) butter, softened
1 cup packed brown sugar
1 cup granulated sugar
2 tablespoons all-purpose flour
4 eggs, lightly beaten
1 unbaked (9-inch) pie shell

Beat the butter in a bowl until creamy. Add the brown sugar, granulated sugar and flour and beat until light and fluffy. Beat in the eggs. Pour into the pie shell. Bake at 350 degrees for 50 to 60 minutes or until set. Remove to a wire rack to cool.

Magnolia Pie

1 1/2 cups sugar
1/4 cup all-purpose flour
5 1/3 tablespoons butter or margarine, softened
3 eggs
1 cup buttermilk
1 1/2 teaspoons vanilla extract
1 unbaked (9-inch) pie shell

Combine the sugar, flour and butter in a bowl. Beat with an electric mixer at medium speed until fluffy. Add the eggs, buttermilk and vanilla. Beat at low speed to mix well. Pour into the pie shell. Bake at 325 degrees for 1 hour or until set. Remove to a wire rack to cool. Garnish with lemon slices and whipped cream.

Pecan Pie

½ cup (1 stick) butter, softened
1 (16-ounce) package light brown sugar
3 eggs, beaten
6 tablespoons milk
2 teaspoons vinegar
3 tablespoons all-purpose flour
1½ teaspoons vanilla extract
1 cup chopped pecans
2 unbaked (9-inch) pie shells
Pecan halves

Mix the butter, brown sugar and eggs in a bowl. Stir in the milk. Stir in the vinegar. Stir in the flour. Stir in the vanilla and 1 cup pecans. Pour into the pie shells. Arrange a few pecan halves on top. Bake at 300 degrees for 1 hour or until set. Remove to a wire rack to cool.

Note: This pie was prepared for our family in Little Washington by Eleanor and Robin.

Pecan Praline Pie

5$\frac{1}{3}$ tablespoons butter or margarine
1 cup sugar
1 cup light corn syrup
4 eggs, lightly beaten
$\frac{1}{4}$ teaspoon salt
1 teaspoon vanilla extract
1 unbaked (9-inch) pie shell
1 cup pecan halves
$\frac{1}{4}$ cup semisweet chocolate chips
$\frac{1}{2}$ cup heavy whipping cream
$\frac{1}{2}$ teaspoon vanilla extract

Melt the butter in a saucepan over low heat. Add the sugar and corn syrup. Cook until the sugar dissolves, stirring constantly. Remove from the heat and let cool slightly. Stir in the eggs, salt and 1 teaspoon vanilla. Pour into the pie shell. Top with the pecans. Bake at 325 degrees for 50 to 55 minutes or until set. Remove to a wire rack to cool completely. Melt the chocolate chips in a microwave-safe bowl in the microwave. Drizzle over the pie. Whip the cream and $\frac{1}{2}$ teaspoon vanilla in a bowl until stiff peaks form. Serve with the pie.

Note: This is one of John's favorites.

Desserts at cherries are truly exceptional—
an art form.

Desserts are made fresh each morning and sell out quickly. Every day is different, enabling us to take advantage of each season's freshest ingredients. We use locally grown fruit whenever it is available, encouraging local farmers to stop by with their harvest.

Our customers can barely get into their seats before they are asking, "What's for dessert?" Something is always just coming out of the oven, making dessert an ever-changing adventure. It is definitely the high point of dining at Cherries.

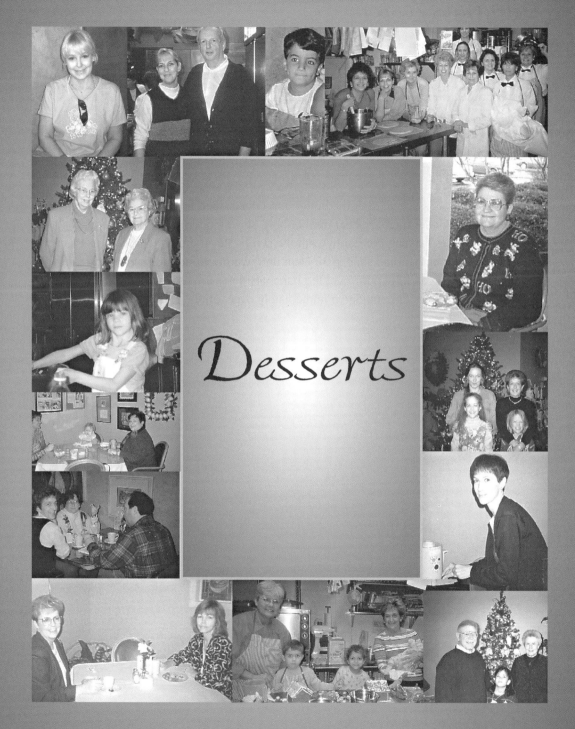

Desserts

Bananas Foster

¼ cup (½ stick) butter or margarine
¼ cup packed brown sugar
½ teaspoon ground cinnamon
4 bananas, quartered lengthwise
1 tablespoon banana extract
¼ cup white rum
Vanilla ice cream

Melt the butter in a large skillet. Stir in the brown sugar and cinnamon. Cook over medium heat until bubbly, stirring often. Add the bananas. Sauté for 2 to 3 minutes, basting constantly with the syrup. Stir in the banana extract. Place the rum in a small long-handled saucepan. Heat until warm; do not boil. Ignite the rum with a long match and carefully pour over the bananas. Baste the bananas with the flaming sauce until the flames die out. Serve immediately over vanilla ice cream.

Banana Shortcake

2 cups all-purpose flour
2 teaspoons baking powder
1/4 teaspoon salt
2 cups sugar
4 eggs
1 cup milk

1/2 cup (1 stick) butter
1 teaspoon vanilla extract
10 bananas
Caramel Sauce
Whipped cream

Mix the flour, baking powder and salt together. Beat the sugar and eggs in a large bowl. Beat in the dry ingredients gradually. Combine the milk and butter in a saucepan. Heat until the butter melts; do not boil. Add to the batter and beat to mix well. Stir in the vanilla, the batter will be thin. Pour into 2 greased and floured 9×11-inch baking pans. Bake at 375 degrees for 20 minutes or until a wooden pick inserted in the center comes out clean. Remove to a wire rack to cool completely. Cut a square of cake and slice in half crosswise. Place the bottom half on a serving plate. Slice 1/2 banana on top. Drizzle with the Caramel Sauce. Top with the other half of the cake square. Slice the remaining 1/2 of the banana on top. Drizzle with the Caramel Sauce and top with whipped cream. Repeat with the remaining cake, bananas, Caramel Sauce and whipped cream. Serve immediately.

Caramel Sauce

1/2 cup (1 stick) butter
1 cup packed brown sugar
1/2 cup heavy cream

Mix the butter, brown sugar and cream in a saucepan. Bring to a boil. Cook for 2 minutes or until the brown sugar is dissolved and the sauce is no longer grainy, stirring constantly. Remove from the heat and let cool.

Bread Pudding

1 (1-pound) loaf French bread or sliced
   white bread
4 cups milk
3 eggs, lightly beaten
1 1/2 cups sugar

1 cup raisins
2 tablespoons vanilla extract
3 tablespoons butter or margarine,
   melted
Whiskey Sauce

     Tear the bread into small chunks and place in a large bowl. Stir in the milk. Let stand for 10 minutes. Mash with hands until well blended. Stir in the eggs, sugar, raisins, vanilla and butter. Spoon into greased muffin cups. Bake at 350 degrees until very firm. Remove to a wire rack to cool. Serve with the Whiskey Sauce.

Whiskey Sauce

1/2 cup (1 stick) butter
1 cup packed brown sugar
1/2 cup half-and-half
2 tablespoons whiskey

     Combine the butter, brown sugar and half-and-half in a heavy saucepan. Cook over medium heat until the sugar dissolves, stirring often. Bring to a boil and reduce the heat. Simmer for 5 minutes, stirring often. Remove from the heat and let cool. Stir in the whiskey.

Chocolate Bread Pudding

1 (1-pound) loaf French bread or sliced
  white bread
2 cups milk
2 cups heavy cream
2 cups sugar
1/2 cup baking cocoa

3 eggs, lightly beaten
1 cup chocolate chips
2 tablespoons vanilla extract
3 tablespoons butter or margarine,
  melted
Chocolate Sauce

Tear the bread into small chunks and place in a large bowl. Stir in the milk and cream. Let stand for 10 minutes. Mash with hands until well blended. Mix the sugar and baking cocoa together. Add to the bread mixture. Stir in the eggs, chocolate chips, vanilla and butter. Spoon into greased muffin cups. Bake at 350 degrees for 30 to 40 minutes until very firm. Remove to a wire rack to cool. Serve with the Chocolate Sauce.

Chocolate Sauce

1/4 cup (1/2 stick) butter
1/2 cup sugar
1/4 cup half-and-half
1 cup chocolate chips

Combine the butter, sugar and half-and-half in a heavy saucepan. Cook over medium heat until the sugar dissolves, stirring often. Stir in the chocolate chips. Bring to a boil and reduce the heat. Simmer for 5 minutes, stirring often. Remove from the heat and let cool.

Chocolate Ice Cream

2 cups sugar
3 egg yolks, beaten
5 to 6 cups milk
4 ounces unsweetened chocolate, melted
1 tablespoon vanilla extract
1 large can evaporated milk

Mix the sugar, egg yolks and 3 cups of the milk in the top of a double boiler. Cook over simmering water until hot but not boiling, stirring constantly. Whisk in the chocolate slowly. Remove from the heat and stir in the vanilla. Stir in the evaporated milk. Pour into a 1 gallon ice cream freezer container. Stir in enough of the remaining milk to fill to the gallon freezer line. Freeze using the manufacturer's directions.

white Chocolate Dream Dessert

Serves 12

24 ladyfingers, split
1/4 cup raspberry liqueur
12 ounces white chocolate, chopped
16 ounces cream cheese, softened
1/4 cup sugar

3 egg yolks
2 teaspoons vanilla extract
3 egg whites
Raspberry Sauce
2 cups heavy whipping cream, whipped

Brush the cut side of each split ladyfinger with the raspberry liqueur. Line the bottom and side of a 9-inch springform pan with the ladyfingers, cut side in. Melt the chocolate in the top of a double boiler over hot water. Stir until smooth. Remove from the heat and let cool. Combine the cream cheese and sugar in a large bowl. Beat with an electric mixer until light and fluffy. Add the egg yolks, 1 at a time, beating well after each addition. Stir in the melted chocolate and vanilla and stir until smooth. Beat the egg whites in a bowl with an electric mixer at high speed until stiff peaks form. Fold into the cream cheese mixture. Spoon into the prepared pan. Cover and chill for at least 8 hours. Pour the Raspberry Sauce evenly over the chilled cream cheese mixture. Top with the whipped cream.

Raspberry Sauce

1 (16-ounce) package frozen
   raspberries, thawed and drained
1/3 cup light corn syrup

1 1/2 tablespoons cornstarch
1 tablespoon raspberry liqueur

Purée the raspberries in a food processor. Push through a wire-mesh strainer into a saucepan and discard the seeds. Add the corn syrup and cornstarch to the raspberry purée. Bring to a boil, stirring often. Cook for 2 minutes, stirring often. Remove from the heat and let cool. Stir in the raspberry liqueur.

Note: If raw eggs are a problem in your area, use an equivalent amount of pasteurized egg yolks and pasteurized egg whites instead of raw eggs.

Crème Brûlée with Raspberry Sauce

Serves 10

4 1/2 cups heavy cream
1/2 cup plus 1 tablespoon sugar
9 egg yolks
1 tablespoon vanilla extract

3/4 cup packed brown sugar, sifted
Raspberry Sauce
1 cup fresh raspberries, or 1/2 (10-ounce)
    package frozen raspberries, thawed

Heat the cream in the top of a double boiler over simmering water. Add the sugar and cook until the sugar dissolves, stirring constantly. Beat the egg yolks in a large bowl until thick and pale yellow. Whisk in the hot cream very slowly. Stir in the vanilla. Strain through a wire-mesh strainer into a shallow 2-quart baking dish. Place the baking dish in a large roasting pan. Add enough very hot water to the larger pan to come 1 1/2 inches up the side of the baking dish. Bake at 300 degrees for 1 hour or until a knife inserted in the center comes out clean; do not overbake. Remove the baking dish to a wire rack and let cool slightly. Sprinkle with the brown sugar. Place under a broiler for 2 minutes or until the brown sugar is melted and bubbly, watching closely so that the sugar doesn't burn. Remove to a wire rack. Pour the Raspberry Sauce over the top and sprinkle with the raspberries.

Raspberry Sauce

1 cup fresh raspberries, or 1/2 (10-ounce)
    package frozen raspberries, thawed

1 tablespoon fresh lemon juice
2 tablespoons sugar

Purée the raspberries in a food processor. Push through a wire-mesh strainer into a bowl and discard the seeds. Stir in the lemon juice and sugar.

Miniature Cheesecakes

16 ounces cream cheese, softened
2 eggs
1/2 cup sugar
2 teaspoons vanilla extract
21 vanilla wafers
1 cup sour cream
2 tablespoons sugar
1/2 teaspoon vanilla extract

      Beat the cream cheese, eggs, 1/2 cup sugar and 2 teaspoons vanilla in a bowl until smooth. Place 1 wafer, flat side up, in the bottom of 21 paper-lined muffin cups. Fill 3/4 full with the cream cheese mixture. Bake at 325 degrees for 15 minutes. Mix the sour cream, 2 tablespoons sugar and 1/2 teaspoon vanilla in a bowl. Spread on top of the baked cheesecakes. Bake for 5 minutes longer. Remove to a wire rack to cool. Garnish with cherries, strawberries, raspberries or shaved chocolate.

chocolate Turtle cheesecake

Serves 12

2 cups crushed vanilla wafers
6 tablespoons margarine, melted
1 (14-ounce) package caramels
1 (5-ounce) can evaporated milk
1 cup pecans, toasted
16 ounces cream cheese, softened
$^1/_2$ cup sugar
2 eggs
1 teaspoon vanilla extract
$^1/_2$ cup semisweet chocolate chips, melted

Mix the crushed wafers and melted margarine in a bowl. Press onto the bottom and up the side of a 9-inch springform pan. Bake at 350 degrees for 10 minutes. Remove to a wire rack to cool. Combine the caramels and evaporated milk in a saucepan. Cook over low heat until melted and smooth, stirring often. Pour evenly over the baked crust and sprinkle with the pecans. Combine the cream cheese, sugar, eggs, vanilla and melted chocolate in a bowl. Beat until creamy. Pour over the pecans. Wrap the outside of the pan tightly with heavy-duty foil. Place the springform pan in a large roasting pan. Add enough very hot water to the larger pan to come halfway up the side of the springform pan. Bake at 300 degrees for 40 minutes. Remove the springform pan to a wire rack and remove the foil outer covering. Let cool completely. Cover and chill.

German Chocolate Cheesecake

1 (8-ounce) package chocolate
   wafers, crushed
6 tablespoons margarine, melted
24 ounces cream cheese, softened
1¼ cups sugar
3 tablespoons cake flour
¼ teaspoon salt

4 eggs
4 ounces German's sweet
   chocolate, melted
¼ cup evaporated milk
1 teaspoon vanilla extract
Topping (below)

     Mix the crushed wafers and melted margarine together in a bowl. Press onto the bottom of a 9-inch springform pan. Beat the cream cheese in a large bowl until light and fluffy. Beat in the sugar, flour and salt gradually. Add the eggs, 1 at a time, beating well after each addition. Stir in the chocolate, evaporated milk and vanilla. Pour into the prepared crust. Bake at 325 degrees for 1 hour. Remove to a wire rack and let cool for 15 minutes. Loosen from the side of the pan with a sharp knife. Let cool for 30 minutes. Remove the side of the pan. Spread with the Topping, leaving 1 inch showing around the outside edge of the cheesecake. Cover and chill for 8 hours.

Topping

2 teaspoons cornstarch
¼ cup sugar
⅔ cup evaporated milk
¼ cup (½ stick) butter or
   margarine, melted

¾ cup chopped pecans
¾ cup flaked coconut
1 teaspoon vanilla extract

     Mix the cornstarch and sugar in a saucepan. Stir in the evaporated milk and butter gradually. Cook over medium heat until the mixture thickens and comes to a boil, stirring constantly. Boil for 1 minute, stirring constantly. Remove from the heat and stir in the pecans, coconut and vanilla. Let cool.

white chocolate and Raspberry cheesecake

18 vanilla wafers

1 cup almonds, toasted

4^{1}/$_{2}$ tablespoons unsalted butter, melted

4 ounces imported white chocolate, chopped

16 ounces cream cheese, softened

^{2}/$_{3}$ cup sugar

2 teaspoons vanilla extract

^{3}/$_{4}$ teaspoon grated lemon zest

2 eggs

^{3}/$_{4}$ cup fresh raspberries or frozen unsweetened raspberries, thawed and drained

1 cup sour cream

3 tablespoons sugar

^{1}/$_{2}$ teaspoon vanilla extract

^{1}/$_{2}$ cup seedless raspberry jam

1 pint fresh raspberries or strawberries

Process the wafers and almonds in a food processor until finely ground. Remove to a bowl. Add the butter. Stir to mix well. Press onto the bottom and 2 inches up the side of a buttered 8-inch springform pan. Bake at 350 degrees for 10 minutes or until golden brown. Remove to a wire rack to cool completely. Melt the chocolate in the top of a double boiler over hot water. Stir until smooth. Remove from the heat. Combine the cream cheese, ^{2}/$_{3}$ cup sugar, 2 teaspoons vanilla and the lemon zest in a large bowl. Beat with an electric mixer until light and fluffy. Add the eggs, 1 at a time, beating well after each addition. Beat in the melted chocolate. Spoon half the cream cheese mixture into the baked crust. Top with ^{3}/$_{4}$ cup raspberries. Spoon the remaining cream cheese mixture over the berries. Bake at 350 degrees for 45 minutes or until the edges are firm but the center is still soft. Remove to a wire rack and let cool for 20 minutes. Press gently on the top of the cheesecake to flatten slightly. Whisk the sour cream, 3 tablespoons sugar and ^{1}/$_{2}$ teaspoon vanilla in a small bowl. Spread over the top of the cheesecake. Bake at 350 degrees for 5 minutes. Remove to a wire rack. Loosen from the side of the pan with a sharp knife. Let cool completely. Remove the side of the pan. Cover and chill overnight. Spread with the jam and top with 1 pint raspberries.

Note: This is a lovely light dessert! It's very impressive.

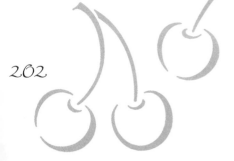

Pumpkin Cheesecake

1²/₃ cups graham cracker crumbs
¹/₂ cup granulated sugar
6 tablespoons butter or
    margarine, melted
24 ounces cream cheese, softened
¹/₂ cup granulated sugar
1 cup packed brown sugar

4 eggs
1 (16-ounce) can pumpkin
1 teaspoon ground cinnamon
¹/₂ teaspoon ginger
¹/₂ teaspoon ground cloves
1 cup heavy cream
Topping (below)

Mix the graham cracker crumbs, ¹/₂ cup granulated sugar and butter in a bowl. Press onto the bottom of a 9-inch springform pan. Chill until cold. Beat the cream cheese in a large bowl until very smooth. Beat in ¹/₂ cup granulated sugar and the brown sugar. Add the eggs, 1 at a time, beating well after each addition. Beat in the pumpkin, cinnamon, ginger, cloves and cream. Pour into the prepared crust. Bake at 350 degrees for 1 hour and 40 minutes. Sprinkle with the Topping. Bake for 10 minutes longer. Remove to a wire rack to cool completely. Cover and chill overnight. Loosen from the side of the pan with a sharp knife and remove the side. Garnish with whipped cream.

Topping

6 tablespoons butter or
    margarine, softened
2 cups packed brown sugar

2 cups coarsely chopped walnuts
    or pecans

Combine the butter and brown sugar in a bowl. Mix until crumbly. Stir in the nuts.

Note: This is a crowd pleaser. It's great at Thanksgiving.

Cranberry Apple Bake

4 cups chopped peeled cooking apples
2 cups fresh cranberries
1 1/2 teaspoons lemon juice
1 cup granulated sugar
1 1/3 cups quick-cooking oats
1 cup chopped walnuts
1/3 cup packed light brown sugar
5 1/3 tablespoons butter or margarine, melted

Mix the apples and cranberries in a lightly greased 2-quart baking dish. Sprinkle with the lemon juice. Sprinkle with the granulated sugar. Mix the oats, walnuts and brown sugar together in a bowl. Add the butter and mix until crumbly. Sprinkle over the fruit. Bake at 325 degrees for 1 hour. Remove to a wire rack. Serve warm with vanilla ice cream.

Fresh Peach Crepes

3 tablespoons Grand Marnier
5 tablespoons sugar
Grated zest of 1 orange
3 tablespoons orange juice
6 large peaches, peeled and sliced
$1/2$ cup blueberries (optional)
1 recipe Crepes (page 28)
Confectioners' sugar

Mix the liqueur, sugar, orange zest and orange juice in a large bowl. Add the peaches and blueberries and stir gently to mix. Let stand for 15 minutes. Lay the crepes on a work surface. Place a spoonful of the fruit in the center of each crepe. Roll up and arrange the crepes in a buttered baking dish. Spoon the remaining mixture over the crepes. Bake at 400 degrees for 10 minutes. Sprinkle with confectioners' sugar before serving. Serve with vanilla sauce, vanilla ice cream or whipped cream.

Meringue Shells with Fresh Fruit

4 egg whites, at room temperature
$1/4$ teaspoon cream of tartar
$1/2$ cup sugar
$1/2$ cup superfine sugar
Ice cream or custard
Fresh fruit

Draw 3-inch circles, 2 inches apart on a foil-lined or parchment-lined baking sheet. Coat lightly with cooking spray. Beat the egg whites in a bowl with an electric mixer until foamy. Beat in the cream of tartar. Mix the sugar and superfine sugar in a bowl. Beat into the egg whites gradually. Beat until stiff peaks form. Spoon the egg white mixture onto the circles on the baking sheet or fill a pastry bag with the egg white mixture and pipe onto the circles. Bake at 250 degrees for 1 hour. Turn off the oven and leave the meringues in the oven for several hours or overnight, do not open the oven door. Remove the meringues and store in an airtight container. Fill with ice cream or custard and top with fresh fruit when ready to serve.

Pecan Tassies

3 ounces cream cheese, softened
7 tablespoons butter, softened
1 cup all-purpose flour
3/4 cup packed light brown sugar
1 tablespoon butter or margarine, softened
1 egg, beaten
1 teaspoon vanilla extract
Dash of salt
3/4 cup chopped pecans

Beat the cream cheese and 7 tablespoons butter in a bowl. Beat in the flour. Divide into 24 portions and shape into balls. Press into the bottom and sides of greased miniature muffin cups. Chill until cold. Beat the brown sugar, 1 tablespoon butter, the egg, vanilla, salt and pecans in a bowl. Spoon into the tart shells, filling 3/4 full. Bake at 350 degrees for 20 minutes or until golden brown. Remove to a wire rack to cool.

Chocolate Fudge Cups

2 cups sugar
3/4 cup baking cocoa
1/2 cup all-purpose flour
5 eggs, beaten
1 cup (2 sticks) butter, melted and cooled
2 teaspoons vanilla extract

Mix the sugar, baking cocoa and flour in a bowl. Add the eggs, melted butter and vanilla. Beat for 3 to 4 minutes or until creamy. Spoon into soufflé cups. Place the soufflé cups in a large roasting pan. Add enough very hot water to the larger pan to come halfway up the sides of the soufflé cups. Bake at 350 degrees for 40 minutes. Remove the soufflé cups to a wire rack to cool completely.

Turtle Volcanos

3/4 cup (1 1/2 sticks) butter
1 cup semisweet chocolate chips
1/3 cup all-purpose flour
3 tablespoons baking cocoa
3 eggs

3 egg yolks
1/3 cup sugar
1 1/2 teaspoons vanilla extract
Praline Sauce (below)
1/3 cup pecans, toasted

Melt the butter and chocolate chips in a saucepan over low heat or melt in a microwave-safe bowl in the microwave. Stir until smooth and let cool. Sift the flour and baking cocoa together. Combine the eggs, egg yolks, sugar and vanilla in a large bowl. Beat until light and fluffy. Beat in the cooled chocolate. Beat in the flour mixture gradually just until combined. Pour into 6 greased and floured 1-cup ramekins. Place the ramekins in a shallow baking pan. Bake at 400 degrees for 10 minutes. Make a dime-size hole in the center of each ramekin. Spoon 1 tablespoon Praline Sauce slowly into each hole. Bake for 5 minutes longer or until firm around the edges. Remove the ramekins to a wire rack and let cool for 3 minutes. Loosen from the side of the ramekin with a spatula. Slip out the volcanoes upright onto dessert plates. Stir the pecans into the remaining Praline Sauce. Spoon over the volcanoes and garnish with whipped cream.

Praline Sauce

1/2 cup granulated sugar
1/3 cup packed brown sugar

2 tablespoons dark corn syrup
1/2 cup heavy cream

Combine the granulated sugar, brown sugar, corn syrup and cream in a saucepan. Bring to a boil, stirring to dissolve the sugar. Cook for 10 minutes or until thickened, stirring occasionally.

crème caramel

2 cups sugar
Juice of 1 lemon
Juice of 1 orange
Water
6 eggs, at room temperature
6 egg yolks, at room temperature
1 cup sugar
2¹/2 cups milk
2¹/2 cups heavy cream
Dash of vanilla extract

Combine 2 cups sugar, the lemon juice and orange juice in a heavy 2-quart saucepan. Add enough water to dissolve the sugar. Stir until the sugar dissolves. Cook over medium heat to a golden to dark brown color. Swirl the pan carefully during cooking, if desired, but do not stir. Pour the boiling sugar mixture carefully into 13 soufflé cups or a 1-quart flan dish. Let cool to room temperature. Combine the eggs, egg yolks and 1 cup sugar in a bowl. Beat gently to mix. Heat the milk, cream and vanilla in a saucepan over medium heat until hot. Whisk gradually into the egg mixture. Pour the custard through a wire-mesh strainer into the soufflé cups or flan dish or pour carefully from the bowl to leave the lumps behind. Place the soufflé cups or flan dish in a large roasting pan. Add enough very hot water to the larger pan to come 1 inch up the side of the cups or flan dish. Bake at 350 degrees for 30 minutes for the soufflé cups or 45 minutes for the flan dish, or until set. Remove the soufflé cups or flan dish to a wire rack to cool completely. Cover and chill until cold.

Note: Rinse the hot saucepan immediately after pouring out the boiling sugar mixture or the pan will be very hard to clean.

Chocolate Peanut Butter Dreams

3 cups rolled oats
1¹/2 cups all-purpose flour
¹/2 teaspoon baking soda
1¹/2 cups packed light brown sugar
³/4 cup (1¹/2 sticks) margarine, softened
1 cup peanut butter

¹/3 cup water
1 egg, beaten
1 teaspoon vanilla extract
1¹/2 cups semisweet chocolate chips
4 teaspoons shortening
¹/3 cup chopped peanuts

Mix the oats, flour and baking soda together. Beat the brown sugar, margarine and peanut butter in a large bowl until light and fluffy. Add the water, egg and vanilla. Stir to mix well. Stir in the dry ingredients. Shape into 1-inch balls. Arrange on an ungreased cookie sheet. Flatten each ball with the bottom of a glass dipped in sugar. Bake at 350 degrees for 8 to 10 minutes or until golden brown. Cool on the cookie sheet for 1 minute. Remove to a wire rack to cool. Combine the chocolate chips and shortening in a saucepan. Cook over low heat until melted and smooth, stirring constantly. Top each cookie with ¹/2 teaspoon of the melted chocolate and sprinkle with the peanuts. Chill until set.

Note: You may melt the chocolate and shortening in a microwave-safe bowl in the microwave, stirring every 30 seconds, instead of in a saucepan.

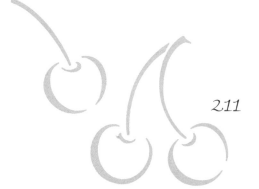

Sugar Cookies

1 cup (2 sticks) butter, softened
1 cup vegetable oil
1 cup granulated sugar
1 cup confectioners' sugar
2 eggs
1 tablespoon vanilla extract
4 1/4 cups self-rising flour

Mix the butter, oil, granulated sugar and confectioners' sugar in a large bowl. Stir in the eggs and vanilla. Stir in the flour. Cover and chill for a few hours. Shape into balls. Arrange on an ungreased cookie sheet. Flatten each ball with the bottom of a glass dipped in melted butter, then sugar. Bake at 350 degrees for 7 to 8 minutes or until light brown. Cool on the cookie sheet for 1 minute. Remove to a wire rack to cool.

Oatmeal Lace Cookies

Makes about 2 dozen cookies

1 1/2 cups (3 sticks) butter
2 cups rolled oats
1 1/2 tablespoons all-purpose flour
1 teaspoon salt
1 3/4 cups sugar
2 teaspoons vanilla extract
2 eggs, lightly beaten

Melt the butter in a large saucepan over low heat. Remove from the heat and let cool slightly. Add the oats, flour, salt, sugar and vanilla. Stir to mix well. Add the eggs and stir to mix well. Spoon 1 1/2 tablespoons of dough, 3 inches apart, on a parchment-lined cookie sheet. Flatten the dough into a circle with the back of a spoon. Bake at 325 degrees for 13 to 15 minutes or just until golden brown. Cool on the cookie sheet for 1 minute. Remove to a wire rack to cool.

Brickle Cookies

1 cup plus 2 tablespoons all-purpose flour
1/4 teaspoon baking soda
1/2 cup (1 stick) butter, softened
1/2 cup granulated sugar
1/4 cup packed brown sugar
1 egg
1 teaspoon vanilla extract
2/3 cup brickle chips

      Mix the flour and baking soda together. Combine the butter, sugar and brown sugar in a bowl. Beat until light and fluffy. Beat in the egg. Beat in the dry ingredients. Stir in the vanilla and brickle chips. Drop by teaspoonfuls onto an ungreased cookie sheet. Bake at 350 degrees for 10 to 12 minutes or until light brown. Cool on the cookie sheet for 1 minute. Remove to a wire rack to cool.

chinese chews

1/2 cup (1 stick) butter or margarine, softened
1 (16-ounce) package brown sugar
3 eggs
1 teaspoon vanilla extract
2 cups self-rising flour
1 (7-ounce) package flaked coconut
1 cup chopped pecans

Combine the butter and brown sugar in a large bowl. Beat until light and fluffy. Add the eggs, 1 at a time, beating well after each addition. Beat in the vanilla. Beat in the flour. Stir in the coconut and pecans. Pour into a greased 11×13-inch baking pan. Bake at 350 degrees for 15 to 20 minutes or until the middle is set. Remove to a wire rack. Cool completely before cutting into squares.

Fudge Oatmeal Bars

¹/₂ cup milk
¹/₂ cup (1 stick) margarine
2 cups sugar
3 tablespoons baking cocoa
Pinch of salt
1 teaspoon vanilla extract
¹/₂ cup peanut butter
3 cups rolled oats

Combine the milk, margarine, sugar, baking cocoa and salt in a saucepan. Bring to a boil, stirring occasionally. Boil for 1 minute. Remove from the heat and stir in the vanilla. Stir in the peanut butter. Add the oats and stir to mix well. Press in a nonstick 9×13-inch baking pan. Let cool and cut into squares.

Note: You may drop the mixture by teaspoonfuls onto waxed paper instead of pressing into a baking pan.

Light Cookies

1 sleeve graham crackers
$1/2$ cup (1stick) butter
$1/2$ cup (1 stick) margarine
$1/2$ cup packed light brown sugar
$1/2$ cup finely chopped pecans

Fit the graham crackers closely together on a foil-lined cookie sheet. Combine the butter, margarine and brown sugar in a saucepan. Bring to a boil, stirring often. Pour evenly over the crackers. Sprinkle with the pecans. Bake at 350 degrees for 10 minutes. Remove to a wire rack to cool completely. Break each cracker into quarters.

Index

221

Cherries Cafe Secrets

Cherries Cafe
6000 Meadowbrook Mall, Suite 2
Clemmons, North Carolina 27012

YOUR ORDER	QUANTITY	TOTAL
Cherries Cafe Secrets at $19.95 per book		$
North Carolina residents add 7% sales tax		$
Postage and handling at $3.95 per book		$
	TOTAL	$

Please make checks payable to Cherries Cafe.

Name
_____

Street Address
_____

City   State   Zip
_____

Telephone
_____

Photocopies will be accepted.